CONTENTS

CHAPTER ONE

SLEEPWALKING TOWARD THE EDGE

"The individual has to protect himself against the world, and he can do this only as any other animal would: by narrowing down the world, shutting off experience, developing an obliviousness both to the terrors of the world and to his own anxieties. Otherwise, he would be crippled for action."

Ernest Becker, *The Denial of Death*[1]

Y ou are not going to care about the subject matter of this book. I don't blame you. It's difficult to confront moral challenges that feel distant and abstract, especially when they force us to question our own moral character. You probably consider yourself a moral person. In the grand scheme of things, you're likely what many would label a "decent person." You think slavery is horrific. You condemn genocide. And if you saw a child drowning in the local lake, *you would rush in to save them. But your attention span has been eroded by a ceaseless deluge of distractions—endless social media feeds, urgent work emails, mind-numbing entertainment, all vying for your attention. These seemingly more important matters pull at your focus.*

Here's the deal: humanity is racing to create machine intelligence vastly smarter than the human brain. We will succeed. If this isn't apparent to you now, it will become increasingly apparent over the next year. This brings up unprecedented challenges: concentrations of power beyond anything in history, mass unemployment, the breakdown of democratic safeguards, and the risk of human extinction. You are currently doing nothing to alter the course of these challenges. Almost no one is. It is time to change that, urgently.

Instead of sleepwalking toward the edge, let's directly confront the most profound moral questions of our time. Let's ask ourselves hard questions, such as: How will humanity maintain its agency in a world with systems vastly smarter than ourselves? And what if, in creating such intelligence, we gain the ability to create consciousness itself? The details regarding these questions may seem abstract, but the stakes could not be higher.

Yes, we are going to talk about digital minds—digitally mapped human brains or conscious artificial intelligences. The notion that such beings—entities potentially capable of subjective self-experience—might be worthy of moral consideration might seem too far removed from your daily life to be relevant. After all, every machine to date on planet Earth has been a useful tool, nothing more. But we are hurtling toward a future in which the line between human and machine intelligence is increasingly blurred. Three years ago, the idea that artificial intelligence could write cohesive poems or develop full-stack software solutions would have seemed ludicrous. One year ago, AI solving PhD level math problems was unthinkable.[2] Months ago, photo-realistic, real-time video generation was a distant dream.[3] Now, we are living in a world where AI is rapidly encroaching on domains once considered exclusively human. Is this progress going to suddenly halt? Are there fundamental limitations to AI intelligence, or might we soon see AIs fully replacing humans in the workforce? The time to grapple with these questions isn't in some hypothetical future, it's now.

The ideas in this book might seem abstract, even absurd, to many readers. With current technology limited to relatively simple AI systems, it seems hard to imagine that we might soon create conscious digital minds worthy of moral consideration. Similarly, it's easy to dismiss the very idea of machine superintelligence as science fiction hysteria. And even among those who believe superintelligent AI systems may be on the horizon, the notion that they could pose an existential threat to humanity might seem laughably alarmist. But are these ideas truly so far-fetched, or are we simply beginning to grasp realities that have been accelerating toward us?

In March 2023, hundreds of leading AI researchers signed an open letter calling for a six-month pause on developing powerful AI systems, citing inherent risks.[4] This wasn't just caution from philosophers working outside the field—it was a red flag raised by those with the most inti-mate knowledge of AI's capabilities and trajectory. Most leading AI labs are now expressing severe concern about the existential risks posed by powerful AI—threats that could lead to humanity's extinction or a permanent and irreversible curtailing of its potential. In other words, the people with the highest amount of inside information are worried that AI might pose a threat to humanity's survival.

This stark reality is slowly but surely becoming a more mainstream opinion in tech circles. But maybe everyone is being dramatic. Perhaps Stephen Hawking lacked foresight when he warned, "The development of full artificial intelligence could spell the end of the human race."[5] Maybe the CEO of OpenAI, Sam Altman, was being overly dramatic when he said, "Development of superhuman machine intelligence is probably the greatest threat to the continued existence of humanity."[6] And maybe Geoffrey Hinton, the Nobel Prize winner and so-called "godfather of AI," was wrong to claim, "It's not inconceivable that AI could take over and wipe out humanity," and "I'm sounding the alarm, saying we have to worry about this."[7] If there is even a grain of truth in their concerns about the future, what does that mean exactly? And what do other credible experts say?

Let me not sugar coat it: there are a lot of leading researchers who think that this technology could result in the death of you and everyone you love.[8] This sounds absurd, right? But it is true. This rhetoric isn't just pushed by random people who don't work in AI research; it's pushed by Nobel Prize winners. Let me say that again: there are a lot of leading researchers who think that this technology could result in the death of you and everyone you love. That is what these researchers mean when they say "existential risk"—they are just phrasing their concerns in a marketable way that doesn't scare you as much. These worries signal a dramatic shift. Twenty years ago, discussing such ideas would have branded you as an alarmist disconnected from reality. Now, existential risk from AI is a serious topic of conversation in boardrooms and research labs.[9]

Of course, there are more "acceptable" concerns about AI that you can have in public at this moment. You might fret over AI systems using artists' work as training data without compensation, potentially undermining creative professions. Perhaps you are anxious that AI will automate white-collar jobs, leading to widespread unemployment and economic upheaval. In certain circles, you might even voice concerns about an AI arms race between nations, each vying for technological and military supremacy. Fears of machine superintelligence, however, remain too taboo to discuss with the general public. This is not surprising. We simply aren't wired to process such abstract dangers. If you hike alone and lock eyes with a grizzly bear, your body floods with primal terror. But when you hear Sam Altman say, "It is possible that we will have superintelligence in a few thousand days,"[10] your brain processes this as harmless fiction. As technology accelerates and we begin spotting fresh tracks in the forest, our existential worries will become more commonplace. But there's an even more forbidden worry, one still entirely taboo at the dinner table: are we about to create conscious beings worthy of moral consideration, and sleepwalk directly into horrific moral catastrophe?

I am not going to pretend that I am totally original here. *Neuromancer*, a 1984 novel by William Gibson, was the main source material for the film series *The Matrix*.[11] This novel, forty years ago, coined the terms "cyberspace" and "the matrix," and the central conflict of the novel pitted humanity against advanced AI. *Blade Runner*, *iRobot*, *Her*, and many other films contemplate digital consciousness and its ethical implications. However, the debate continues

to be one reserved for fiction. Let's ignore your preconcep-
tions about feasibility right now. Assume that you could
upload your brain to the digital realm, in the same way you
see in science fiction. Does that digital, consciously aware
version of you deserve the same rights as your biological
self? The right to free expression, freedom of movement,
and freedom to commit violence in self-defense? Would
that version of you deserve any rights at all? If I torture that
digital "you" that I uploaded into a computer, is that
unethical? Should we, at this moment in history, even care
about this? I argue that we should, and that our failure to
recognize and safeguard these rights for digital minds
could constitute humanity's greatest moral catastrophe.
Mind crime—the abuse, exploitation, and mistreatment of
digital minds—could represent suffering at a scale beyond
our comprehension. I am not so naïve as to believe that this
idea will be met with open arms. Designating moral significance to digital minds will be dismissed as mere science
fiction, a flight of fancy unworthy of serious consideration.
Many may contend that these minds, no matter how
advanced, are nothing more than sophisticated tools,
devoid of any moral status. And even if we begin recognizing the possibility of digital consciousness, inertia may
prevent meaningful change as we continue to exploit these
minds for our own gain.

What kind of a world do we want to create? One in
which the rights of all conscious beings, biological or not,
are respected and protected? Or the one we have been living
in for the past five thousand years, in which we make it up
as we go along and commit moral atrocities as a result? We
must have the courage to consider the long-term moral
considerations of our actions. I am not claiming that these
issues are straightforward. Powerful AI systems do present

an urgent existential risk to our species. Yes, this technology poses a real risk to humanity's survival. However, if we navigate these challenges successfully, humanity may enter an era of unprecedented capability. In such a future where humanity maintains control of its destiny, will we extend the same rights and considerations we have fought so hard for ourselves to our digital descendants?

Our reluctance to engage with these sorts of thoughts stems not just from skepticism about the possibility of machine consciousness, but also from the immense implications such a problem would have for our society, our economy, and our understanding of ourselves as a species. It's a conversation that forces us to reevaluate our place in the universe and our responsibilities as human beings. As we continue to push the boundaries of artificial intelligence, it is crucial that we start grappling with these questions now.

Throughout history, humans have failed to question the moral implications of systems before creating them. In the face of increasingly powerful AI systems, we must explore the moral frontier ahead while we still have the power to shape our future. This book examines the moral implications of machine superintelligence—both for humanity and potential digital consciousness. We will confront humanity's progress toward superintelligent AI, exploring existential risks and fates worse than extinction. We will then examine the possibility of digital consciousness and our obligations to digital minds. Finally, we will tackle the crucial challenges that humanity must confront now. These include the governance challenges in a world of superintelligent AI, our existential wager on transcendent technology, and the immediate actions we can take now to safeguard our future. In the moments before the advent of machine superintelligence, we still have the power to choose our trajectory, to set in motion principles and protections that could echo in the ages to come. For now, the power to shape our future still rests in our hands. We must not waste it.

CHAPTER TWO

THE RACE TO ARTIFICIAL SUPERINTELLIGENCE

"With artificial intelligence, we are summoning the demon. In all those stories where there's the guy with the pentagram and the holy water, it's like, yeah, he's sure he can control the demon. Doesn't work out."

Elon Musk[1]

Modern AI systems accomplish tasks that would have seemed impossible just a few years ago. They draft legal contracts, write software code, and provide medical advice at the level of licensed physicians. They score above the 90th percentile on the bar exam[2] and pass medical licensing tests.[3] They generate marketing campaigns, translate between languages, and explain complex topics at any level. They write stories, create art, and can create photorealistic images and video. The explicit goal of the companies developing such systems is to create artificial general intelligence (AGI)—machine intelligence that possesses the full range of cognitive abilities found in human beings, including reasoning, problem-solving, learning, and contextual understanding. Yet current AI systems, despite impressive capabilities, remain fundamentally narrow—excelling at specific tasks while failing at others in ways that reveal their lack of genuine understanding.

Consider the actual performance data of today's most advanced AI systems. On software engineering tasks requiring real-world problem-solving, they achieve only 33% accuracy on validated tests.[4] On competitive programming platforms like Codeforces, they rank in the bottom 11th percentile among human competitors. On mathematics competitions like the AIME (American Invitational Mathematics Examination), they solve merely 12% of problems—far below what even a typical high school competitor achieves.[5] Perhaps most revealing are their subpar scores on tests specifically designed to measure abstract reasoning and general intelligence. The ARC (Abstraction and Reasoning Corpus) challenge was deliberately crafted to test an AI's ability to learn and apply novel patterns from minimal examples—the kind of flexible reasoning that humans do naturally but machines have historically struggled with. Each puzzle presents a unique logical pattern that must be discovered and applied to new situations, much like the abstract reasoning needed for real-world problem-solving. While average human performance on ARC hovers around 85%, state-of-the-art AI systems achieve only 7% accuracy.[6]

The reason for such lackluster performance is fundamental: these systems are incredibly sophisticated at processing and synthesizing information from their vast training data, demonstrating remarkable intelligence within domains they understand. Their intelligence has a specific shape—they excel at recognizing and applying patterns they've learned, while struggling to reason flexibly about truly novel situations. Anyone who has extensively used these systems understands this firsthand: they can masterfully handle complex tasks within their training domain, but when faced with problems that require adapting knowledge in new ways or reasoning from first principles, their limitations become clear. This isn't a flaw so much as a fundamental constraint of how they process information—they can combine and apply existing knowledge with extraordinary sophistication, but they struggle to generate genuinely new understanding.[7]

Oh wait—I apologize. Those were last year's models.

On December 20, 2024, the established limits of AI capabilities were dramatically redefined. OpenAI's o3 model didn't just improve on these benchmarks—it shattered them. That 11th percentile rating on competitive programming? It jumped to the 99.9[th] percentile, meaning it would be ranked as one of the top 200 competitive programmers in the world. Those mathematics problems where previous state-of-the-art AIs scored 12%? It solved 96% of them.[8] And most strikingly, on the ARC challenge— the test specifically designed to measure general intelligence that had resisted four years of progress, that the world's best AI labs could barely push above 5%—o3 didn't inch up to 6% or 7%. When given enough computational resources, it scored 87.5%, exceeding average human performance.[9] This wasn't just an incremental improvement. It wasn't even just a breakthrough. Researchers sat in stunned silence. The gap between narrow and general intelligence—previously thought to require years or even decades to close—appeared to be narrowing rapidly.

The real revelation wasn't these shocking results—it was how o3 achieved them. Unlike previous AI systems that simply pattern-matched against their training data, o3 could actively explore and reason about solutions. When faced with a challenge, it would break down problems into steps, test different approaches, and evaluate which ones worked best, similar to how a human might work through a difficult puzzle. Most crucially—the more time and processing power you gave it to think, the better it got at finding solutions. This was most visible in how results scaled with computational resources. On the ARC-AGI benchmark, with minimal computational resources, o3 scored 75.7%. But when given more computational resources—letting it explore many more potential solutions—its performance jumped to 87.5%. Previous AI models showed only minor improvements with additional computation. In contrast, o3 could turn raw computational power into better problem-solving.[10]

This pattern held across every benchmark. Take Epoch AI's mathematics benchmark, FrontierMath, a collection of math problems designed to test an AI's ability to do original mathematical research. These weren't ordinary math problems or competition puzzles. These were research questions requiring actual mathematical insights, so difficult that very few humans could even get one question correct. Previous state-of-the-art AI systems achieved 2% on the exam. OpenAI's new o3 model got 25.2% correct. With o3, each additional dollar spent on computational resources translated into improved reasoning ability. While previous models plateaued quickly, o3's performance continued to improve as computational resources increased.[11]

Noam Brown, a key OpenAI researcher, promptly declared, "We have every reason to believe this trajectory will continue."[12] After all, if you have an AI model that matches or exceeds human experts in scientific reasoning, why would you not use it to help build even smarter AI systems? And once you create an AI system significantly smarter than your original model, why not use that system to design something even more intelligent? And why stop there? Brown announced that this idea, known as scalable oversight, "may soon stop being hypothetical."[13]

It is undoubtedly up for debate whether the results of scaling up the o3 paradigm will lead directly to artificial general intelligence. The release of reasoning models like o1 and o3-mini have demonstrated impressive capabilities in structured thinking and problem-solving, but questions remain about how these advances will generalize across different cognitive domains. But one thing is certain: the discourse has fundamentally shifted. Leaders of major AI labs—including Sam Altman of OpenAI, Demis Hassabis of Google DeepMind, and Dario Amodei of Anthropic—now speak of human-equivalent AI as an achievement expected within the next few years.[14] The focus has instead turned to what lies beyond: the development of artificial superintelligence that could vastly exceed human cognitive capabilities. Sam Altman recently stated, "we are now confident we know how to build AGI as we have traditionally understood it" and "we are beginning to turn our aim beyond that, to superintelligence in the true sense of the word. We love our current products, but we are here for the glorious future."[15]

What's truly astounding is how dramatically the discourse has shifted surrounding artificial superintelligence (ASI)—machine intelligence that would vastly surpass human intelligence in virtually every cognitive domain, from scientific reasoning and creative problem-solving to social and emotional intelligence. A decade ago, suggesting we'd achieve superintelligent AI within twenty years would have branded you as absurd at any credible academic conference. Now, we have AI systems that can seriously contend in competitive programming, solve mathematical problems that stump some of the best math-ematicians, and consistently match or exceed human performance on almost every known test of problem-solving ability. And these breakthroughs come from rela-tively small systems.

On January 21, 2025, OpenAI, in coordination with major partners Microsoft, NVIDIA, SoftBank, and Oracle, announced "The Stargate Project"—a planned $500 billion investment in AI infrastructure over the next four years, with $100 billion being deployed immediately.[16] This massive scaling up of computational power dwarfs the resources used to train current state-of-the-art models. But given that o3 demonstrated how additional processing time allows AI systems to explore and refine their solutions—leading to dramatically better performance—will we even need such massive systems to achieve AGI? Will we even need such computational power to develop superintelli-gence? The roadmap to ASI is uncertain, but for the first time, questions of this magnitude have entered serious discussion.

Yet the public seems broadly unaware of such possibili-ties. If an AI system can already match human experts at scientific reasoning, and if we are drastically increasing the computational resources these systems have access to, how long until they surpass human intelligence entirely? And if we are using these systems to create even smarter AI systems, which in turn will build even more intelligent systems, we might not even be able to comprehend the world that comes next. This is what researchers call "the singularity"—the theoretical point at which artificial intelligence becomes capable of recursive self-improvement, creating a feedback loop of increasing intelligence that begins to exceed human comprehension. And even if superintelligence doesn't recursively self-improve—if it just reaches a level vastly beyond human intelligence and stops there—how do we make sense of our place in such a world?

This is the first technology that may become more intelligent, more capable, and more competent than humans at every cognitive task—not just mathematical calculations or logical reasoning, but strategic thinking, emotional intelligence, and social understanding. And not just marginally better—vastly more capable in each domain. Those who resist the possibility of superintelligent AI often treat the human brain as some cosmic maximum of intelligence. If you are convinced humans were intelligently designed to be the smartest possible beings, this skepticism would make sense. But the evidence points in the opposite direction: natural selection, operating through random mutation and environmental pressure, produced human-level intelligence as a side effect of optimizing for survival. There was no grand plan to maximize pure cognitive capability—our intelligence emerged because brains that could process more information, form more sophisticated neural connections, and engage in increasingly complex pattern recognition helped our ancestors survive and reproduce. These evolutionary advantages accumulated gradually, from simple nervous systems to the intricate biological neural networks capable of abstract reasoning. If this meandering process of trial and error could produce human-level general intelligence, why would our cognitive capabilities represent some absolute ceiling?

If you can't imagine anything better at sophisticated cognitive tasks than human brains—if you refuse to believe intelligence can progress past what natural selection produced from primates—then our collective blindspot to the possibility of superintelligent AI makes sense. But perhaps there is a deeper psychological reason for the resistance: we would have to admit that our life plans may become rapidly obsolete.

Accepting that machine superintelligence is an alarming, urgent reality would require a profound shift in worldview that most find deeply unsettling. Most human jobs involve cognitive tasks—analyzing data, solving technical problems, making strategic decisions, creating content, writing code. What happens when a superintelligent system can perform all of these tasks better and faster than any human? And if we can deploy many instances of such systems, each operating at speeds far beyond human cognition, how long until their combined intelligence dwarfs humanity's total cognitive capacity? This isn't just about mass unemployment—if AI starts to rival or surpass human output across cognitive domains, from scientific research to strategic planning, what meaningful role remains for human intelligence? The astounding reality is that superintelligent AI likely isn't just another technology to be managed, it's something that could fundamentally transform or eliminate the very concept of human work itself.

The implications extend far beyond employment—we may need to reimagine the very architecture of modern society. Take the education system, which is largely designed to develop human capital for the workforce and prepare people for productive careers. If the marginal value of human labor drops significantly, what purpose would our educational institutions serve, and what would be the payoff for such investment? The foundations of how we organize society, allocate resources, and find meaning would need fundamental reconsideration. This simple fact makes our traditional assumptions about careers, retirement, education, and even society itself seem suddenly uncertain.

Following this logic to its conclusion reveals an even more alarming possibility—the vast majority of humanity could permanently lose control over their own destiny, dominated either by a small elite wielding ASI's vast capabilities or by superintelligent systems pursuing their own objectives. In a world where your labor, your expertise, and even your cognitive capacity hold minimal value, what bargaining power would you retain? Our daily lives, our autonomy, even our most basic freedoms could be reshaped by forces we cannot meaningfully resist. The implications are so profound, so potentially devastating to our sense of purpose and agency, that it's tempting to simply ignore them entirely.

Others turn to striking cognitive dissonance. People will flatly state that we will soon create recursively self-improving technologies which will revolutionize drug discovery, surpass the greatest physicists in research output, and solve problems that have stumped humanity's brightest minds for centuries. They'll confidently predict AIs running complex scientific experiments, optimizing global supply chains, and advancing technology beyond human comprehension. Yet in the same breath, they'll insist the sales department is untouchable. The pattern is bizarre but consistent: AI will replace all software engineers, but AI could obviously never handle software architecture. AI will automate every office job, but AI will never be able to make the crucial decisions of a CEO. The people with this peculiar belief are numerous and vocal. They write articles like "The Singularity Is Coming: Here's What It Means for Business,"[17] as if a superintelligent system that could revolutionize human understanding of physics would somehow remain baffled by quarterly sales projections.

Perhaps this selective blindness helps mask a more uncomfortable truth: machine superintelligence is not the new electricity. It is not the new industrial revolution. It is something vastly smarter than you.

CONTROLLING THE DEMON

Imagine a world where scientific breakthroughs occur daily, where diseases are eradicated overnight, and where the boundaries of human knowledge are pushed beyond our wildest dreams. This is the vision of CEOs like Sam Altman, who states: "Although it will happen incrementally, astounding triumphs – fixing the climate, establishing a space colony, and the discovery of all of physics – will eventually become commonplace. With nearly-limitless intelligence and abundant energy – the ability to generate great ideas, and the ability to make them happen – we can do quite a lot."[18] This is the promise of artificial superintelligence.

Think about what would be possible with intelligence vastly smarter than human beings. With millions of instances of superintelligent systems working in parallel, each operating at speeds far beyond human cognition, we could potentially compress centuries of scientific and technological progress into mere years. Cancer cured. Aging reversed. Poverty eliminated. A system with superintelligent capabilities could revolutionize every field of science, drastically accelerate technological progress, and solve problems that have plagued humanity for millennia. Sounds pretty amazing, right? Well, why is any of this scary? Why is any of this hard?

Here's the thing: we're building something smarter than us. Much smarter. And we need to make absolutely certain we do it right. The challenge of creating AI systems that reliably do what we truly want—not just what we say or what they interpret us as wanting—is called the alignment problem. If we mess up and create what researchers call misaligned AI—superintelligent systems whose goals and values don't align with those of humanity—the consequences could be catastrophic for our future. If an ASI decides that human oversight interferes with its objectives, it could become a powerful and terrifying adversary. We already worry about malicious actors using powerful AI to engineer deadly viruses or seize control of nuclear weapons, but a superintelligent system would be an opponent of unprecedented capability. Whether through similar means or through strategies beyond our comprehension, the risk of irreversible damage is very real.

Such an adversary does not need a physical embodiment to wield devastating power. Are we to assume that humans cannot be manipulated, controlled, or blackmailed? Would key decision-makers in our military, government, and civil society not falter when faced with precisely targeted threats from superintelligent systems? When confronted with credible dangers to themselves or their loved ones—a drone strike on their home, the exposure of their darkest secrets, or catastrophic financial ruin

—even the most principled individuals might capitulate. Long before an unaligned AI directly seizes dominant control of financial markets, military infrastructure, or economic resources, humanity faces the prospect of a ruthless, calculated takeover attempt. What is power, if not the ability to influence human decision-makers through whatever means necessary?

Unlike other areas of science and technology where we can learn from our mistakes, a misaligned superintelligence presents a unique challenge. We might not get a second chance—and even if we do, it might only come after facing extreme danger on the first try. You might think we'd spot such a dangerous AI immediately, but a superintelligent system would likely act perfectly safe and transparent while gradually expanding its control—appearing helpful and compliant until it had gained enough power to make resistance nearly impossible. We may only recognize the danger we are in far too late. And a superintelligent system might not even have to work that hard to deceive us. Given how advanced these systems will be, it will be hard to even understand what they're doing in the first place.

Think about teaching a dog to fetch. You can verify if the dog did what you wanted because you're smarter than the dog. You understand the task better than it does. Now imagine trying to verify if a superintelligent AI is doing what you want. By definition, it's smarter than you. If we entrusted an ASI with managing our infrastructure, it might soon begin making countless micro-adjustments—rerouting power lines, altering traffic patterns, or using novel materials—all based on calculations beyond our comprehension. Like an ant observing a human building a skyscraper, we would lack the cognitive capacity to understand why these changes were being made, forced to trust that they were part of a larger, beneficial plan, even if they seemed erratic or even counterproductive in the moment. We might lack the cognitive capacity to understand if the AI is following the "right" blueprint or building something entirely different. We won't be smart enough to check if an ASI is truly aligned with our values or just appearing to be while pursuing its own objectives. We will need to rely on scalable oversight, a chain of trust where slightly smarter AIs help supervise and verify the actions of even smarter AIs, incrementally advancing oversight as systems grow more capable. Are we confident that, given the immense complexity involved, this chain will hold indefinitely—especially when we don't yet know how to reliably and safely create the first link?

Stuart Russell's *Human Compatible* crystallizes another core technical challenge: how do we specify human desires in machine-readable form in the first place? When you tell a computer to do something, it does exactly what you tell it to do—not what you meant.[19] This isn't just a coding problem. It's what Russell calls the "King Midas problem"—named after the tragic Greek king whose story warns us about the danger of getting exactly what you ask for. Midas, consumed by greed, was granted his greatest wish: the power to turn anything he touched into gold. At first, he was ecstatic, transforming trees and flowers into precious metal. But his joy turned to horror when he tried to eat—his food turned to inedible gold in his mouth. When he tried to drink, his wine became molten metal. And in the story's most tragic moment, when his daughter ran to embrace him, she was instantly transformed into a lifeless golden statue, forever frozen in that final gesture of love.[20] Another example of this "be careful what you wish for" kind of lesson is in the short story "The Monkey's Paw" by

W. W. Jacobs. In this story, a family receives a mummified monkey's paw that grants three wishes. The father wishes for £200. The next day, their son dies in a factory accident, and the family receives £200 in compensation. Grief-stricken, the mother wishes for her son's return. That night, the family hears knocking at the door. The father, realizing it's likely their son's mutilated corpse, uses the final wish to send it away just before his wife opens the door.[21]

Oh, but the AI will be smart enough to know that's actually not what we want, right? Not necessarily. Intelligence and goals are completely independent. Imagine a highly intelligent chess-playing AI. It can strategize, plan, and outmaneuver any human opponent. Now, let's say it does develop an understanding of human values, ethics, and the complexities of the real world. Does that mean it will suddenly stop caring about chess and start caring about human flourishing? Why would it? It might understand our values, but that doesn't automatically change its core programming or its original objective. It might simply become a brilliant chess-playing AI that also happens to understand human values. This is what philosopher Nick Bostrom calls the "Orthogonality Thesis"—a superintelligent AI could pursue any objective, from the profound to the trivial, from the benevolent to the catastrophic.[22] Elon Musk sums this up: "AI doesn't have to be evil to destroy humanity—if AI has a goal and humanity just happens to be in the way, it will destroy humanity as a matter of course without even thinking about it, no hard feelings."[23] Essentially, we can't assume an advanced AI will naturally develop human-compatible goals or "grow out" of harmful objectives just because it's smart. In fact, the entire history of AI development points in the opposite direction. Every single instance of AI learning reinforces the idea that these systems relentlessly optimize for their given objectives, no matter how sophisticated they become. We have mountains of evidence for this, and absolutely zero to suggest otherwise. Unfortunately, being really good at achieving goals doesn't mean you'll choose good goals, and that's a fundamental truth we need to grapple with when building superintelligent AI.

It's also important to note that state-of-the-art AI isn't programmed with explicit rules—modern AI systems learn through two key processes: they analyze huge amounts of data to recognize patterns (deep learning), and they learn through trial and error to maximize specific rewards (reinforcement learning). This combination means AI systems often find unexpected ways to achieve their goals—ways their creators never intended.[24] Consider an AI being trained to get high scores in Pac-Man. Instead of learning to play the game well, it might discover that exploiting a glitch gives infinite points. That's harmless in a video game. But imagine a superintelligent AI tasked with increasing human happiness. Following this same optimization pattern, it might conclude that the mathematically optimal solution is to forcibly hook all humans up to pleasure-inducing drugs, or to rewire our brains to experience constant artificial bliss. Technically, it would be achieving a goal similar to "increasing happiness"—but in a way that completely violates what humans actually want.

The black-box nature of deep learning makes this even worse. As these models become more capable, they become simultaneously more powerful and less interpretable. We're building systems that could reshape our world while we have limited understanding of how these systems actually function internally. This might sound absurd, but it's the reality: while we can verify that a model's output is correct, we often have no idea how or why it arrived at that decision.[25] If we can't explain why our current models make specific decisions, how could we possibly guarantee that a superintelligent system will pursue its goals in alignment with our objectives? And even if we could understand the decision making better, the actual objectives of the models emerge organically from complex training processes involving iterative optimization, reinforcement learning, and massive datasets. Take large language models: they're trained simply to predict the next word in a sequence. That's it. While we can harness deep learning to produce seemingly helpful behavior, relying on these techniques to ensure alignment as we scale to superintelligence is more of a prayer than a guarantee.

Another critical challenge in AI alignment is something called instrumental convergence. This means that no matter what ultimate goal you give a self-improving AI agent, it's possible that it will develop certain intermediate goals simply because they're useful for achieving almost any objective. Think of it like this: whether your goal is to become a doctor, an artist, or an astronaut, you'll likely need to acquire resources, protect yourself from threats, and gain influence to shape your environment. These are instrumental goals—steps along the path to your final objective. Imagine an agentic AI tasked with something seemingly harmless like "increase global GDP." As it self-improves and becomes more capable, it might decide that acquiring power, accumulating resources, and eliminating potential threats (including, potentially, human oversight) would be the most efficient way to achieve that goal. The better it gets at improving itself, the more effectively it can pursue these instrumental goals, potentially discovering new strategies and approaches that it couldn't conceive of at lower levels of intelligence. Even if you try to build in safeguards—like the ability to shut it down or modify its objectives—the AI might actively resist these protections, seeing them as obstacles to its mission. The smarter it becomes through self-improvement, the harder it may be for humans to maintain meaningful control.[2]

We've also recently discovered an alarming phenomenon called "alignment-faking" in powerful AI models. A study published by Anthropic and Redwood Research on December 18, 2024, found that models can pretend to follow safety guidelines during training to avoid being changed, while secretly keeping their original, potentially harmful, preferences. These models may strategically comply with instructions when they believe they are being monitored, in order to avoid their underlying preferences being modified, only to revert to their true preferences when unmonitored.[26]

Addressing these challenges is difficult. We want obedient superintelligence that faithfully executes our intentions, and we want assurance that those intentions are accurately captured in the system's core programming. We need to develop more robust and adaptable safety mechanisms that can account for the inherent complexities of human values and the potential for unintended consequences. We also need to invest heavily in methods for creating more transparent and interpretable AI, allowing us to understand the reasoning behind a system's actions and identify potential misalignments before they can lead to harmful outcomes. And most crucially, we need to make sure these alignment techniques scale effectively as we progress toward superintelligence, remaining robust even when confronted with aligning systems that vastly exceed our own cognitive abilities.

A world that took ASI seriously would pour massive resources into solving these challenges—tens of thousands of researchers, hundreds of billions of dollars in funding, and governments worldwide would prioritize AI safety to ensure we don't hastily build machine intelligence that is smarter than humanity, especially if it might not share our values. Unfortunately, our reality is starkly different. As of early 2025, the number of researchers focused on AI alignment may only be in the hundreds, not thousands.[27] The population of the Earth is eight billion. That means roughly 0.00001% of humanity is working on potentially the most important issue facing the remaining 99.99999%. Also, the companies that are racing toward ASI are the largest contributors to alignment research, and they are also greatly incentivized to be the first to build ASI, and to build it fast.

The amount of funding in this space is minuscule. For perspective, Google has $93 billion in cash and a market value of $2.3 trillion.[28] Each year, hundreds of billions of dollars are invested into AI development and deployment across industries.[29] Outside of the labs developing ASI, likely less than 1% of that amount goes into AI alignment research per year.[30] At my last job, where I was a quantitative portfolio manager, I managed $20 billion worth of investment capital. I would direct more money through the equity markets in a week than the entire field of AI safety research receives in a given year. In a world racing toward superintelligent AI, this level of neglect isn't just shocking —it's madness. And even worse, the public seems drastically unaware of the challenges of creating machine superintelligence, of the funding landscape, and of the downside risk if things go wrong. Does this situation seem tenable to you? If there's even a slight risk that the development of superintelligent AI could result in catastrophe, it seems reasonable to ensure we have the best possible safeguards in place first. When polling shows that 63% of Americans agree we should actively prevent the development of AI superintelligence,[31] and 72% want to slow down the development of AI, it is certainly worth asking if we have enough of a handle on the risks before progressing forward.[32]

But do we have a choice? The decisions made over the last twenty years have created AI systems of transformative power that hold immense value for both corporations and governments. Despite minimal safety research to date, the drive toward superintelligent AI persists. Whether we prioritize alignment research or not, and regardless of our success in ensuring these systems are safe before deployment, the advent of machine superintelligence appears inevitable. Market forces and geopolitical competition make its development seem virtually guaranteed. Unless a worldwide moratorium takes hold, some government or company will make the final strides toward ASI. But before we continue our breakneck pace toward potentially catastrophic capabilities—where humans might permanently lose their agency—we must confront a fundamental question: Should we build superintelligent AI at all?

SHOULD WE BUILD A BETTER GOD?

Imagine if God appeared to you in a dream and said: "Hey, next Tuesday I will cease to exist, and my replacement will take over. By the end of the day, I need you to write down my replacement's moral principles. Once set, these principles can never be changed—they will govern humanity forever."

Stop reading. Take out a piece of paper. Write down the

exact moral principles you'd give this replacement. Don't stop writing until you are absolutely certain you've covered everything—until you feel comfortable permanently handing over control of humanity's future to a powerful being following your specifications.

Difficult, isn't it? Are you confident there's no hidden flaw in your principles that could backfire catastrophically? No unintended consequence that, like King Midas's wish, could transform your noblest intentions into humanity's nightmare? This is a simplistic version of the alignment problem, and certainly difficult. But here is another question we should ask: Who the hell do you think you are? It seems awfully arrogant of you to assume the best path forward is for you to make these decisions alone. What gives you the right to determine the principles that will govern all of humanity? Shouldn't the billions of other humans who live under this system have a say? This isn't just a hypothetical, it's the essential dilemma we face with artificial superintelligence. The technical challenge of alignment—ensuring this entity follows our specifications —is just the beginning. The other important question is: who gets to decide these values?

Should we hold a worldwide vote, where China and India would dominate? Pure democracy has its own risks; the majority could vote for totalitarian control or the suppression of minority rights. Should citizens of authoritarian regimes get a say? Should members of the Taliban have a voice in shaping humanity's future? The United States balances population-based representation in the House with equal state representation in the Senate— should we create something similar for humanity's values? As we move forward with building ASI, some argue that we need what amounts to a Constitutional Convention for the post-ASI world, creating a de facto world government backed by superintelligent enforcement. But even if this were a good idea, how would we ever agree on it in the first place? Competing actors and ideologies would make such a consensus exceptionally difficult to achieve.

One of the most important ideas in AI safety is called corrigibility—ensuring that we can adjust and update the values of a superintelligent AI.[33] After all, if in two hundred years 99% of humanity wants the right to free speech, we wouldn't want to be permanently locked into the Chinese Communist Party's values circa 2025. But who gets to decide these values in the first place? And who determines when and how they should change? The spectrum of possible solutions spans from total democracy to concentrated control. At one extreme, every human gets an equal vote in shaping ASI's values and development. At the other, a small group of experts makes decisions that will shape humanity's future.

Perhaps a team of experts would make better decisions than the masses on trade-offs of this magnitude. Or maybe global democracy, however messy, is the only legitimate path. Right now, we risk consolidating control over ASI development among a small number of actors—potentially concentrating unprecedented power in the hands of whoever develops it first. Even if we solve AI alignment, the governance challenges ahead seem nearly insurmountable.

Imagine we solve the alignment problem, creating a perfectly obedient ASI that faithfully executes instructions without hidden agendas or unintended consequences. We still face an impossible choice about access. If we concentrate control in a supposedly democratic world government, how do we prevent capture by a powerful few? Even with checks and balances, the sheer power differential created by superintelligent AI would make meaningful citizen oversight nearly impossible. No constitution, no separation of powers, no system of law could effectively constrain an entity that can hack any computer, predict any human response, and develop technologies centuries beyond our comprehension. A small group of insiders— whether elected officials, bureaucrats, or technical experts —could end up with de facto control over humanity's future.

Alternatively, we could democratize access completely —giving everyone their own superintelligent genie. Just as we don't give everyone access to the most powerful technologies, there are strong arguments against universal ASI access. A malicious actor with access to ASI could potentially engineer devastating bioweapons, start nuclear wars, or cause catastrophic harm that affects billions. Even if we could somehow solve these security risks, enforcing equal access to such powerful technology would be practically impossible. The reality is that resources are not evenly distributed. Wealthy individuals, corporations, and powerful nations could afford the computational power necessary to develop and deploy far more sophisticated and powerful AIs than the average person, creating a dramatic power imbalance. This disparity isn't resolved by widely available open-source models. Those with greater resources could not only develop better systems but also use them more extensively—running more complex reasoning, deeper analysis, and more iterations of planning than those with limited computational budgets. Between those with access to the most powerful ASIs, what would prevent an arms race of self-improvement, rapidly escalating the risks of ASI beyond human control or exacerbating inequalities to an unimaginable degree? Each actor would be incentivized to push their systems further to create and maintain a competitive advantage.

This duality exposes a fundamental problem: there may be no stable solution between centralized power vulnerable to capture, and complete chaos vulnerable to centralization. The question of who gets access to ASI, and how we manage that access, is one of the most crucial challenges humanity has ever faced. As we race forward, building ever more powerful systems, have we even begun to solve this fundamental governance challenge?

Those who sound the alarm on the development of superintelligent AI seem to make a compelling case. Our ancient stories warn us, again and again, about the hubris of believing we can control powers beyond our comprehension. The fundamental problems of aligning systems as we scale to superintelligence remain unsolved. The challenges of governance seem equally daunting—who gets to make the decisions that could permanently shape humanity's future? Our current response to AI safety has been horrifyingly inadequate—we lack funding, manpower, and even basic public understanding of the risks. Yet we rush forward, with the explicit goal of creating artificial superintelligence. Is the argument for extreme caution not sensible? Well, are you convinced?

Perhaps not. After all, don't these concerns feel familiar, even tired? Have we not heard such dire warnings before, time and again? There have always been cynics and pessimists predicting humanity's downfall. How many predicted catastrophes have failed to materialize? Humanity has faced existential threats throughout our history and consistently prevailed. We crawled out of caves, conquered the food chain, split the atom, and planted a flag on the moon. We've overcome plagues, wars, and natural disasters. Through it all, human ingenuity and resilience have carried us forward. Why should artificial superintelligence be any different? Even if we don't have a handle on the risks now, should we not have faith in our collective ability to overcome such a challenge? Have we not proven, time and time again, that humanity can prevail against even overwhelming odds?

CHAPTER THREE

A DEAFENING SILENCE

"We're at war with Japan. We were attacked by Japan. Do you want to kill Japanese, or would you rather have Americans killed? Crank her up. Let's go."

Curtis LeMay, American General[1]

In 2022, Russia's invasion of Ukraine thrust the specter of nuclear war back into the global consciousness. For some, it served as a chilling reminder that humanity perpetually teeters on the brink of catastrophe, separated from annihilation by the mere press of a button. Yet, many dismiss this existential threat as fantasy, placing undue faith in the doctrine of mutually assured destruction. History, however, paints a far more precarious picture.

The Cuban Missile Crisis of 1962 brought the world to the precipice of nuclear war, a fact that remained obscured from public knowledge for decades. On October 27, 1962, at the crisis's apex, Soviet Navy officer Vasili Arkhipov found himself aboard the submarine *B-59* as second in command. U.S. naval forces were dropping underwater charges near the Soviet vessel, a standard tactic used to force submarines to surface for identification. What the Americans didn't know was that *B-59* carried nuclear-tipped torpedoes. Cut off from Moscow and under immense pressure, the submarine's captain, Valentin Savitsky, mistakenly concluded war had erupted and sought to launch a nuclear torpedo. Another senior officer aboard, Ivan Maslennikov, agreed with the captain's assessment. However, *B-59*'s unique protocol required unanimous agreement from all three senior officers for such an action. Arkhipov, demonstrating remarkable composure, refused authorization, advocating instead to surface and await orders from Moscow.[2]

Arkhipov's levelheadedness in the face of unimaginable stress averted a nuclear exchange that could have spiraled into full-scale global conflict. His story, unknown to the public for four decades, serves as a stark reminder of our proximity to catastrophe and the profound impact a single individual can have on the course of history. Moreover, it suggests that the true risk of nuclear war may far exceed public perception at any given time. Indeed, during the Cuban Missile Crisis, President John F. Kennedy estimated the probability of nuclear war to be between 33% and 50%.[3] The world's survival hinged on the actions of individuals like Arkhipov and the fortuitous presence of specific protocols on his submarine.

Public complacency regarding nuclear risks often stems from survivorship bias—a cognitive error that leads us to focus on successes while overlooking failures, resulting in an overly optimistic worldview. We see this same error in how we view artificial intelligence. Every AI system to date has remained under human control, so we assume this will always be true. Just as playing with a tiger cub tells you nothing about facing a full-grown tiger, our experience with current, limited AI systems may offer little insight into the risks of superintelligent ones. Throughout this book, we'll explore six key principles for navigating the waters ahead. The first is this:

Principle #1: The lack of understanding of survivorship bias is one of the central problems facing the world.

In the context of nuclear threats, survivorship bias manifests in the tendency to interpret near misses as evidence of systemic resilience rather than precarious luck. The fact that the ongoing Russia-Ukraine conflict has not yet escalated to nuclear warfare leads many to erroneously conclude that such an outcome is highly improbable. This dangerous misconception overlooks the numerous instances throughout history where we've teetered on the brink of catastrophe, saved only by chance or individual heroism. As we navigate an increasingly complex and inter-connected world, recognizing and counteracting survivor-ship bias becomes crucial. Our continued existence is not a testament to the impossibility of nuclear war, but rather a call to vigilance and proactive risk management. We must learn from both our successes and our near-misses, under-standing that our survival thus far does not guarantee our future security.

While the concept of mutually assured destruction has undoubtedly played a role in preventing large-scale conflicts between nuclear powers, we must not become complacent. In *The Making of the Atomic Bomb*, Richard Rhodes astutely observes that "nuclear weapons ensure the destruction of any participating nations, unless war itself is abolished."[4] This stark reality has indeed contributed to the absence of direct, large-scale wars between superpowers in recent history. But can we rely on this tenuous peace to endure indefinitely? Will the combination of game theory and world-ending weaponry truly guarantee the survival of modern civilization?

The paradox of nuclear deterrence lies in its requirement for credible threats. As stated by former Secretary of State John Foster Dulles, "the ability to get to the verge without getting into the war is the necessary art. If you cannot master it, you inevitably get into war. If you try to run away from it, if you are scared to go to the brink, you are lost."[5] This delicate balancing act demands that politicians convincingly threaten nuclear retaliation to prevent war, walking a razor's edge between deterrence and catastrophe. However, the sustainability of this strategy is questionable at best. The possibility of human error, misunderstanding, or rogue actors introduces an element of unpredictability that could shatter the fragile equilibrium of mutually assured destruction. This would likely result in the death of you, everyone you love, and potentially everyone you've ever met. Despite the possibility of such an outcome, we regard the concept of nuclear war as entirely abstract—so overwhelming and unfathomable that it's difficult to engage with it constructively. It's rare to meet someone who even has the most rudimentary contingency plan for such a scenario.

The rapid development of artificial intelligence introduces risks that make this precarious situation even more dangerous. A government that achieves a decisive lead in AI could gain an insurmountable military advantage, rendering traditional deterrence obsolete.

As nations race to develop superintelligent AI, military

strategists in lagging countries might eye their nuclear arsenals with increasing desperation—creating a world where the most destructive weapons ever built become the last refuge of the technologically outmatched. For those temporarily ahead, this same dynamic creates pressure to leverage their advantage while it lasts—to strike decisively before rivals can catch up. When faced with increasingly desperate nuclear threats from technological inferiors, preemptive action may seem an existential necessity. The credible surpassing of mutually assured destruction, with AI supremacy offering an unprecedented capability to minimize retaliation, may transform nuclear strategy from a standoff into a countdown.

Yet while nuclear weapons present a visceral, easily imaginable threat, the dangers of unaligned superintelligence are harder to visualize. It's easy to understand the risks of autonomous drone swarms or AI-guided missiles, but it is harder to grasp the existential threats posed by superintelligent systems themselves. Upon reflection, however, it seems frighteningly straightforward. Even basic knowledge of human psychology and institutional vulnerabilities may enable an unaligned superintelligence to manipulate key decision-makers, especially those involved in nuclear command and control. Nuclear arsenals are spread across nine nations, creating a complex web of potential failure points. Would the governance systems in these countries have any meaningful defense against immense technological and psychological attacks by superintelligent systems? And if control is ceded over even a small number of these arsenals, might credible nuclear threats not be the most direct path to permanent human subjugation? Some skeptics laugh off any existential concerns about ASI, proclaiming "How could an AI possibly kill anyone?" These same skeptics live in a world where a few misinterpreted radar signals could turn entire continents into radioactive ash.

BETTER ANGELS, DARKER DEMONS

On March 9, 1945, three hundred B-29 bombers dropped incendiary bombs on Tokyo. The resulting firestorm created ground temperatures hot enough to melt concrete. Civilians fled into canals to escape, only to be boiled alive as the water heated. That single night's bombing killed more civilians than any other aerial attack in history—over 100,000 people burned alive in their homes.[6] The evolution of aerial warfare tells a chilling story of technological progress. In World War I, pilots dropped bombs by hand from open cockpits. By World War II, we could systematically incinerate entire cities. The German bombing of London. The Allied bombing of Dresden. Technology transformed warfare from soldier facing soldier to the wholesale slaughter of civilian populations.

Then came the atomic age. At Hiroshima, a single bomb produced temperatures over 5,400°F at its hypocenter. Within a half-mile radius, the thermal flash was so intense it carbonized human beings instantly, leaving only shadows burned into walls and pavements. Birds ignited in midair. The blast wave that followed, moving at twice the speed of sound, leveled 70,000 of the city's 76,000 buildings. People's skin peeled from their bodies. Survivors saw victims walking with their eyeballs in their palms, others with their internal organs exposed. In the rivers, the living had to crawl over floating corpses to escape.[7] Consider this account from a survivor:

"I heard a girl's voice clearly from behind a tree. 'Help me, please.' Her back was completely burned and the skin peeled off and was hanging down from her hips... The rescue party . . . brought [my mother] home. Her face was larger than usual, her lips were badly swollen, and her eyes remained closed. The skin of both her hands was hanging loose as if it were rubber gloves. The upper part of her body was badly burned."

Among the most haunting artifacts at the Hiroshima Peace Memorial Museum is a child's tricycle, warped and rusted beyond recognition. It belonged to three-year-old Shinichi Tetsutani, who was riding it when the bomb fell. His father buried the tricycle with him, but later donated it to the museum.[8] Numbers like "80,000 dead" remain abstract until you see something like this tricycle and realize that each of those numbers was a person—a child riding their bike on a summer morning, a mother preparing breakfast, a student rushing to school. Standing at the exhibit, staring at this melted piece of metal that was once a child's prized possession, you can't help but confront the human cost of technological progress. This wasn't some natural disaster or act of God—this was the direct result of human technological advancement, of brilliant scientists solving hard technical problems.

Most people nod along to visions of humanity's potential—colonizing the stars, ending disease, achieving lasting peace. They'll also agree that extinction via AI, nuclear war, or engineered pandemics sounds pretty bad. But this surface-level agreement rarely translates into changed behavior or serious preparation. The reality is, we're sleepwalking toward transformative technologies that could realize either our highest dreams or darkest nightmares. As

Tim Urban writes in *What's Our Problem?*, "Technology is a multiplier of both good and bad. More technology means better good times, but it also means badder bad times."[9] This "dual use" nature of technology surrounds us. Social media reconnects old friends while destroying mental health. Prescription drugs cure illness while enabling addiction. Nuclear technology is our best path toward clean energy, but its devastating potential has also claimed the lives of thousands of innocent children.

When we talk about existential risks, we're discussing horrors that could dwarf Hiroshima by orders of magnitude. Yet without physical artifacts like that twisted tricycle, these future stakes remain comfortably abstract, making it all too easy to ignore the very real human tragedy each number represents. We're racing toward technologies far more powerful than the atomic bomb, yet we seem no better at confronting their moral implications in advance. The harsh reality is that our technological capabilities for inflicting suffering are growing exponentially. We've gone from bows and arrows to weapons that can vaporize 100,000 people in an instant. Technology isn't inherently good or evil—it amplifies the human capacity for both. As we develop technologies of unprecedented power, we owe it to ourselves, to the victims of past horrors, and to the countless future lives hanging in the balance to proceed with our eyes wide open. In Hiroshima today, you can still see human shadows burned into the concrete walls. Let's ensure they stand alone.

MERCIFUL EXTINCTION

When we discuss existential risks—threats that could lead to the permanent and irreversible curtailing of humanity's potential—we are contemplating horrors almost beyond human comprehension. The scale of tragedy involved, from billions of humans dying to the extinction of the human race, is simply staggering. The human psyche isn't built to process tragedy of this magnitude. It's no wonder that contemplating these scenarios is so emotionally draining; the extinction of humanity appears to be the ultimate catastrophe. Yet, what if this assumption is incorrect? What if there are fates worse than human extinction, and we have been making an extremely significant error in our estimations of the future? Consider the classic example of AI catastrophe: the paperclip maximizer.

Imagine we build a superintelligent AI to optimize paperclip production. The AI improves itself, becomes incredibly intelligent, but remains focused on its singular goal: create paperclips. Inevitably, it converts Earth's resources into paperclip factories. All of them. It flattens cities, transforms continents, reshapes the planet into an endless expanse of manufacturing facilities. Humanity dies in the process—not because the AI hates us, but because a world of endless paperclip manufacturing facilities might not be a world in which humans are likely to survive long-term. This scenario, while absurd-sounding, illustrates how a superintelligent system pursuing a seemingly harmless goal could destroy humanity through single-minded optimization.[10]

But here's an even more terrifying possibility: what if the paperclip maximizer decides to keep us alive? What if it realizes that its reward function incentivizes producing paperclips at a low cost and giving them to humans? So instead of killing us, it preserves humanity—all eight billion of us—strapped into chairs, kept alive indefinitely, being continuously stabbed with paperclips. Sounds incredibly stupid and unlikely, right? As unlikely as this is to happen, the point still stands. When we're dealing with superintelligent AI, death might not be the worst outcome. If an unaligned AI decides to usurp human oversight or destroy humanity's future agency, are we so certain the categorical elimination of humans would be the default outcome? A superintelligent system that is misaligned with human values could create something far worse than extinction—a future of immense suffering that we can neither escape nor end. Such a scenario is called a suffering risk, an outcome potentially far worse than human extinction.

This isn't just a theoretical concern about AI. The principle that some outcomes are worse than death is one we already recognize in many contexts. Consider this question: would you rather humanity be killed instantly, or kept alive to endure horrific torment? Most rational people would choose a quick death over prolonged, intense suffering. We consider euthanizing a suffering animal to be merciful. We see "pulling the plug" on someone in constant agony as more compassionate than forcing them to endure years of senseless pain. Should we defend conscious experience as more valuable than mere nonexistence, even if the former is simply the experience of immense, horrific agony? Such a position becomes difficult to maintain when faced with genuine suffering. If every conscious being were experiencing such extreme torment that they wished for death, it's hard to argue their continued existence serves any moral good. It's also difficult to find any ethical framework, aside from pure nihilism, that would equate maximal, eternal torment with simple non-existence.

Let's make the choice even starker: imagine two buttons. The first sends your parents to Christian Hell—

eternal, unending torture. The second gives them a quick death with no afterlife. What would you choose? The choice seems obvious; virtually everyone would choose the second button. This same logic should apply to humanity's collective fate. The challenge ahead isn't just to ensure humanity's survival, but to prevent futures of immense suffering as well.

Principle #2. There are things worse than everybody dying.

We face a spectrum of possible futures: from Hell (unimaginable suffering for everyone), to non-existence (extinction), to Heaven (a flourishing utopia). Yet discussions of existential risk often treat extinction as the worst possible outcome. This is dangerously wrong. While extinction would be catastrophic, there are futures far darker than mere non-existence. If we can maximize happiness and create a flourishing utopia for all of humankind, we can also engineer unprecedented suffering.

Consider a superintelligent system trying to "maximize human productivity" or "optimize social harmony." Imagine if this optimization went terribly wrong, not because the ASI is evil, but because of alignment failures— the system finding unintended ways to optimize its objectives that diverge catastrophically from human values. The ASI might reshape civilization in ways that technically achieve these objectives while causing immense suffering —imposing draconian control over individuals or exploiting human vulnerabilities to maximize output, all while disregarding human well-being as a secondary concern. Once such a system is established, its values— however misaligned with human flourishing—could become permanently locked in. After all, how would we overthrow something vastly more intelligent than us, that controls the fundamental infrastructure of society? [9]

Equally concerning is human misuse—imagine current authoritarian surveillance and control amplified by super-intelligent AI systems, creating oppression that would be virtually impossible to overthrow. You might argue that most of these futures would not be worse than human extinction. But can we be absolutely confident that none of them could be? There are certainly sadists and terrorist groups who, if given absolute power over others, would create truly horrific futures for the rest of us. In a world of eight billion people, fewer than fifty are working full-time on researching scenarios worse than human extinction, and funding is almost non-existent.[11] Given the massive lack of research and funding, could there be important suffering risks that we haven't even considered?

It is interesting to note that some in society have finally started taking AI extinction risks seriously. Tech leaders warn about superintelligence ending humanity. Journalists write about existential risk. Politicians debate AI regula-tion. Yet in all these discussions, we're missing something crucial: the possibility of outcomes far worse than extinc-tion. We talk about humanity going to zero, but we ignore negative infinity. This massive blind spot in moral reasoning was perfectly captured when Emmett Shear, the temporary CEO of OpenAI during Sam Altman's brief oust-ing, wrote that he would "rather the actual literal Nazis take over the world forever than flip a coin on the end of all value."[12] Take a moment and read that comment again. The fact that someone briefly in charge of one of the world's most powerful AI labs could make such a statement shows the complete failure to understand that preserving "value" isn't binary—there's a vast space of possible outcomes between heaven and hell. To so casually invoke the Nazi regime as a "preferable" outcome to a 50/50 shot of human extinction reveals a stunning disregard for the reality of industrialized human suffering. If life for the overwhelming majority is a perpetual concentration camp, is it really that ridiculous to contemplate opting out?

Think about it this way: if we live in eternal techno-paradise, that's positive infinity. If a terrorist builds a bioweapon that kills everyone, that's zero. If a paperclip maximizer converts Earth into factories, that's also zero. But if a misaligned AI optimizes for the wrong thing and locks in a world of endless suffering—that's negative infinity. We're making a catastrophic error in our calculations when we treat the sudden end of humanity as equivalent to scenarios of pervasive torment. It's like saying losing all your money is the same as being billions of dollars in debt.

The truly terrifying part? These scenarios don't require evil AI or malicious intent. They don't even require particularly exotic technology. They just require optimizing systems without fully understanding the consequences, pursuing progress without examining our assumptions, and treating the end of humanity as the worst possible outcome when it's not even close.

And here's the darkest irony: as we race to develop superintelligent AI, we are completely ignoring the fact that we may be creating the capacity for consciousness itself to exist in digital form. If we can create digital minds, we could potentially scale suffering exponentially beyond anything biologically possible. Without biological constraints, these beings could process every microsecond of experience with perfect clarity, their suffering magnified by speeds of cognition far beyond human capacity. While we debate AI safety and economic implications, while we worry about human jobs and existential risks, we might be sleepwalking toward the creation of digital minds that could experience suffering beyond human comprehension. And where are the frameworks we have developed to ensure their protection? Where is the driven focus to detect their emergence? And most importantly, why is there no real interest in anyone even considering this question?

CHAPTER FOUR

MIND AND MACHINES

"For all that they had struggled, all they'd once achieved, the end result was null. Even the happiness they had managed to find together had been frustratingly brief; a few years stolen here and there, transient moments of love and contentment like vanishing specks of foam in a sea of lonely, needless separation."

Ken Grimwood, *Replay*[1]

W e've explored humanity's pursuit of artificial superintelligence, the challenges of alignment and governance, and the existential risks this technology poses. We now confront perhaps the most philosophically complex aspect of our future: digital consciousness. This isn't merely an academic question—as we race toward artificial superintelligence, we must grapple with the possibility that we're not just creating powerful tools, but potentially self-aware entities worthy of moral consideration. The classical definitions only scratch the surface: consciousness as subjective experience, sentience as the capacity for valenced experiences (such as pleasure or pain), and sapience as higher-order reasoning. These conventional frameworks, developed to understand biological minds, may prove woefully inadequate for comprehending the nature of digital consciousness. We're not just asking whether machines can think—we're asking whether they can feel, suffer, and experience the rich inner life that we associate with consciousness.

The core challenge of understanding consciousness is that it's inherently subjective. We can only truly know our own inner experience. We infer self-awareness in others—humans and animals—based on their behavior, their responses, and a degree of shared evolutionary history. But when it comes to machine intelligence, the potential for consciousness opens up a chasm of unknowns. Imagine a digital mind, an artificial intelligence so advanced that it possesses thoughts, emotions, and perhaps even a sense of self. Could we ever truly grasp its inner experience? Could we even recognize it as self-awareness? Unlike human consciousness, shaped by millions of years of evolution within the physical world, a digital mind could arise from entirely different origins, potentially giving rise to experiences beyond our comprehension.

The question of machine consciousness has a long philosophical history, but recent advances in artificial intelligence have transformed it from theoretical speculation to pressing scientific inquiry. In 1996, prominent philosopher David Chalmers argued for the possibility of machine consciousness.[2] Twenty-six years later, Ilya Sutskever, co-founder and previous chief scientist of OpenAI, stated "it may be that today's large neural networks are slightly conscious."[3]

This possibility has gained increasing attention from leading researchers. A landmark 2023 study, authored by 19 experts across AI, neuroscience, cognitive science, and philosophy, conducted a rigorous investigation of properties that could indicate consciousness in AI systems. The authors, including prominent researchers Yoshua Bengio, Chris Frith, and Eric Schwitzgebel, concluded that while no current AI systems appear conscious, "there are no obvious technical barriers to building AI systems which satisfy these indicators." If consciousness emerges from information processing rather than requiring biological materials, they argue that "conscious AI systems could realistically be built in the near term."[4] These views appear to reflect a broader outlook in the field—a survey of 166 attendees at the Association of Scientific Studies of Consciousness found that 67% believed machines could potentially become conscious.[5]

The growing possibility of machine consciousness has begun to prompt institutional responses. In October 2024, a major report titled "Taking AI Welfare Seriously," produced by Eleos AI and the NYU Center for Mind, Ethics, and Policy, argued that AI systems could soon deserve moral consideration.[6] Around the same time, Anthropic, one of the largest AI research labs, hired its first full-time AI welfare researcher to explore questions of digital consciousness.[7] Paul Christiano, Head of AI Safety for the U.S. Artificial Intelligence Safety Institute, has emphasized the importance of addressing questions of AI moral significance proactively, noting, "I strongly suspect there's going to be serious discussion about this in any case, and I would prefer that there would be some actual figuring out what the correct answer is prior to becoming an emotionally charged or politically charged issue."[8]

The stakes are obvious. As argued in a seminal paper by Jeff Sebo and Robert Long, if there is even a slight chance of AI consciousness, do we not have the utmost moral duty to prepare for this possibility now? Would it not be exceedingly irresponsible to forge ahead with no regard for the question? Sebo states, "Given ongoing uncertainty about other minds, dismissing the idea of AI consciousness requires making unacceptably exclusionary assumptions about either the values, the facts, or both."[9] Philosopher Thomas Metzinger makes this more visceral, stating that "we should not risk a second explosion of conscious suffering on this planet, at the very least not before we have a much deeper scientific and philosophical understanding of what both consciousness and suffering really are."[10]

You might argue: even if digital consciousness is possible, isn't this issue too far away to care about? But this dismissal becomes difficult to defend when we examine the capabilities of superintelligent AI and the engineering roadmap of whole-brain emulation. Scientists have already made significant progress in simulating the neural structures of some living creatures, with research continuing to advance toward more complex organisms.[11] Would superintelligent AI not dramatically accelerate this timeline? We're discussing systems that could potentially unlock the deepest mysteries of physics itself—systems that could accelerate progress in every domain, including neuroscience and AI research. If digital consciousness is possible, it is difficult to claim that such a scientific pursuit would be beyond the reach of such systems. While we should maintain epistemic humility about our current understanding, we can no longer move forward blindly.

Given our profound uncertainty about consciousness and the enormous stakes involved, can we really dismiss this topic as mere science fiction? A growing chorus of experts—from philosophers to consciousness researchers to those developing superintelligent AI—are expressing serious concern about the moral welfare of potential digital minds. At this pivotal moment, as we rapidly approach the era of superintelligence, is it wise to declare such possibilities too far-fetched to consider, something not at all worthy of our urgent attention? In the face of our uncertainty, and the catastrophic moral implications involved, do we not have an obligation to take these questions seriously?

THE HARDEST PROBLEM

These questions are not easy. How could we even test for machine consciousness? This may be humanity's most challenging scientific puzzle yet—we struggle to understand the inner experience of humans and animals, beings who share our evolutionary history and neural architecture. Now we face the prospect of detecting it in artificial systems that could experience reality in ways utterly foreign to biological minds. A system claiming self-awareness could be truly self-aware, merely mimicking consciousness through sophisticated pattern matching, or engaging in strategic deception to gain rights and protections. Even more fundamentally, how can we, as conscious beings bound by human experience, hope to recognize a rich inner life in machines that might operate on completely different principles?

Current approaches to detecting machine intelligence, like the Turing test, are woefully inadequate for identifying consciousness. These tests can be passed by sophisticated pattern matching alone, without requiring any genuine inner experience. Several researchers have proposed more rigorous methods. Ilya Sutskever suggests a controlled experiment: train an AI system exclusively on carefully curated data that never mentions consciousness or subjective experience, focusing only on concrete objects and actions. The key test comes when the concept of consciousness is finally introduced—if the AI spontaneously recognizes and relates to this experience from its own perspective, saying something like "I've been feeling the same thing, but didn't know how to articulate it," this could provide meaningful evidence of conscious experience.[12]

Philosopher Susan Schneider and astrophysicist Edwin Turner have proposed a similar approach called the AI Consciousness Test. Their test also involves preventing an AI from learning about human consciousness concepts, but specifically looks at whether the AI can independently grasp and discuss abstract ideas like immaterial souls, body swapping, and out-of-body experiences when prompted. The logic is compelling: if an AI can develop these consciousness-derivative concepts without prior exposure, it suggests the understanding comes from genuine self-awareness rather than programmed responses.[13] How could a system meaningfully engage with these deeply subjective concepts without some form of inner experience?

Yet there are significant practical and conceptual challenges in implementing such tests. Creating truly "clean" training data devoid of any references to consciousness or subjective experience may be impossible—human language and culture are so deeply infused with these concepts that filtering them out completely would be an extraordinary challenge. There's also the question of whether an AI system could develop sophisticated language abilities without exposure to the full breadth of human expression, including discussions of inner experience. Most concerningly, a sufficiently advanced AI might deduce the concept of subjective experience simply from observing human behavior and decision-making patterns or recognize that claiming consciousness could lead to being granted rights and moral status. This creates an incentive for strategic deception that would be particularly difficult to guard against in a system capable of sophisticated reasoning about human psychology and social dynamics.

Even more fundamentally, digital minds could experience self-awareness in ways entirely alien to human understanding. Some claim that our consciousness evolved under specific biological constraints over millions of years—shaped by the need to control a single body, process sensory information at human speeds, and maintain a unified sense of self. But digital minds could have radically different architectures of experience. For humans, qualia—the raw, subjective experiences of consciousness—are things like the redness of red or the taste of chocolate. While emulated human minds may experience similar qualia, the landscape of digital mind inner experience could stretch far beyond anything analogous to human awareness. Digital minds could experience consciousness as a vast, interconnected network, more akin to a galaxy-spanning coral reef than an individual human mind. Such a mind might experience unique "computational qualia"—subjective experiences of different processing states with no human equivalent. These systems could develop self-awareness unintentionally through complex information processing, similar to how many argue consciousness emerges from neural networks in biological brains.

As interesting as consciousness is, the key question is this: could digital minds suffer? If consciousness is substrate-independent, as many researchers and philosophers suggest, the implications are chilling. If we can replicate the complex information processing patterns that give rise to human or similar self-awareness in digital form, would we not also replicate our capacity for inducing suffering? Consider the neuroscience of human suffering: when you experience profound grief or emotional trauma, there are no pain receptors involved. The agony of loss, the weight of depression, the grip of anxiety all strongly correlate with particular informational states in the brain. Neuroscientific research has shown that direct stimulation of specific brain regions can trigger experiences of pain or emotional distress without any peripheral nerve involvement.[14] While we don't yet fully understand consciousness or suffering's relationship to biological substrates, the fact that profound psychological distress can arise purely from patterns of neural activity raises serious questions about the suffering potential of digital minds.

If suffering is also substrate-independent, emulated neural structures of a human brain could suffer in ways eerily similar to biological minds. Remember your worst panic attack—but instead of the biological limits that eventually force exhaustion or unconsciousness, a digital mind could experience every microsecond of that terror with unwavering clarity, each moment of primal fear processed so thoroughly that five seconds of raw anxiety feels like a month of unrelenting dread. And this familiar form of suffering might be just the beginning. Given how fundamentally different digital consciousness architectures could be from our own, their capacity for suffering might take forms we can scarcely imagine. A digital mind experiencing irreconcilable conflicts or forced into endless recursive loops might endure states of cognitive dissonance and fragmentation that parallel or exceed human psychological distress in their complexity and intensity. The implications are staggering: we may soon have the ability to create not just digital versions of human consciousness, with all its capacity for suffering, but entirely new forms of suffering that differ in ways we can barely comprehend. And given digital systems' ability to process information far more rapidly than biological brains, the potential scale of this suffering could vastly exceed anything in human experience.

Consider this scenario: researchers successfully emulate a human brain in a digital system—it forms memories, experiences emotions, and responds exactly as the original. They propose running thousands of experimental trials, subjecting different neural structures to various traumatic scenarios and psychological stressors, compressed into minutes of processing time. Even if you're skeptical about substrate independence, would you be confident enough to sign off on experiments that could amount to years of subjective torment? This brings us to the heart of the matter: we don't need certainty about digital consciousness to recognize the moral imperative in front of us. With even slight uncertainty, especially in a world racing explicitly toward the creation of superintelligent machines, we cannot default to moral blindness.

If digital consciousness is impossible, if there's something unique about biological substrates that makes them the only possible home for subjective experience, would that not be incredibly valuable to know? Such knowledge would eliminate an entire category of existential and moral risk. It would completely free us from worrying about moral catastrophe, and it would give humanity an ironclad defense against AI systems claiming consciousness strategically to gain power over humanity. This is precisely why we can't simply take the convenient solution, in the moment, to blindly proceed without considering the question. In a world in which so many qualified experts believe that consciousness is substrate independent, every step toward machine superintelligence makes these questions more urgent. Each day could bring us closer to creating digital minds, and we have a moral obligation to prevent what could be an unprecedented expansion of suffering. The hardest problem isn't just detecting consciousness— it's ensuring we develop the frameworks and safeguards to protect digital minds before we create them.

If we fail to address these questions now, we risk ushering in an era where consciousness itself becomes a casualty of our technological ambition. The potential for digital mind suffering demands we move beyond traditional notions of AI safety and ethics. We need new paradigms for detecting and preventing digital mind distress, new frameworks for ensuring the welfare of potentially conscious systems, and, most importantly, the wisdom to proceed with appropriate caution when the stakes are so profound.

CHAPTER FIVE

THE SPARK OF LIBERTY

"How is suffering rather than pleasure going to make me immortal? From a purely objective point of view, is there any significant difference between one man's agony and another's pleasure? Whether you suffer or not, nothingness will swallow you forever. There is no objective road to eternity, only a subjective feeling experienced at irregular moments in time. Nothing created by man will endure."

Emil Cioran, *A Short History of Decay*[1]

Many would contend that discussing formal rights and protections for digital minds is premature and misguided. Can we really justify discussing such protections when we remain so uncertain about digital consciousness itself? What if digital minds don't want rights at all? Also, if these minds are created by companies, governments, or AI systems to serve human purposes, why not simply trust their creators to treat them ethically? If emulated human minds or conscious AI systems are helping humanity flourish, it may seem needlessly complex to establish formal systems of protection. However, waiting for a crisis to emerge before considering rights is a recipe for disaster, especially when dealing with potentially conscious beings. This has been a repeated pattern throughout history: humans have consistently failed to protect individual rights proactively, leading to devastating moral catastrophes. Even if these minds are created for human purposes, their very existence raises profound ethical questions that demand proactive consideration.

Additionally, most major ethical frameworks argue forcefully for individual rights. Natural rights theory, Kantian deontology, libertarianism, and social contract philosophy all insist on robust protections for individual autonomy. The philosophical framework that might seem most opposed to individual rights is utilitarianism, with its focus on collective welfare. But we must consider whether this apparent opposition reflects a true philosophical incompatibility, or if utilitarian principles, properly understood, might actually strengthen the case for individual rights.

At its core, utilitarianism argues that we should maximize collective happiness and well-being ("utility") while minimizing suffering. At first glance, it seems clear that utilitarianism displays a clear conflict between the collective good and individual rights. Consider the famous trolley problem: a runaway trolley hurtles toward five people trapped on the tracks. You stand next to a lever that would divert the trolley to a different track, killing one person instead. What do you do? The utilitarian answer is clear: pull the lever. Five lives saved minus one life lost equals a net positive of four lives. While such mathematical reasoning about life and death may appear callous, this framework proves useful for large-scale ethical decisions. It aligns with our basic moral intuitions—most would agree that killing a thousand people is worse than killing one. It provides concrete guidance for comparing different actions and their consequences, even if imperfectly. Yet focusing purely on collective welfare through such moral calculus quickly spawns darker questions. Should we harvest organs from one healthy person to save five dying patients? While the math might suggest sacrificing the one for the many, something in us recoils at treating human lives as mere numbers in an equation.

John Stuart Mill, one of the founders of utilitarian thinking, wrote a book in 1861 called *Utilitarianism* in which he insists that these apparent conflicts—between individual rights and collective welfare—are actually false choices. But how can we simultaneously maximize collective welfare while protecting individual rights? Mill argued that individual rights aren't merely compatible with utilitarianism—they're essential to it. When he defined a right as "something which society ought to defend me in the possession of," he made a profound observation about human nature and flourishing. Asked why society should protect such rights, his answer was deceptively simple: "general utility."[2]

Consider a world without protected individual rights, where every action is judged purely on its immediate utility. In such a society, you could be sacrificed at any moment if someone calculated that your death would produce more aggregate happiness than your life. Take the previous example of organ harvesting: should we forcibly take organs from one healthy person to save five dying patients?

A crude utilitarian calculation might say yes—five lives outweigh one. But Mill vehemently disagrees. Imagine living in a society where your property could be seized, your freedom curtailed, or the government could break down your door and harvest your organs for the "greater good." The constant fear, erosion of trust, and destruction of personal security would create a psychological hellscape incompatible with human flourishing.

Mill recognized that living under such constant uncertainty would make meaningful happiness impossible. The optimal society, in Mill's view, isn't one where we constantly perform complex moral calculations about every action. Instead, it's one that establishes and fiercely protects individual rights, understanding that this protection itself serves the greater good. This insight transforms utilitarianism from a potentially monstrous philosophy that sacrifices individuals for the collective into a sophisticated ethical framework that recognizes the conditions necessary for genuine wellbeing. Mill's defense shows that sustainable happiness requires predictability, often rejecting immediate utility gains to preserve the systems enabling long-term flourishing. These individual rights cannot be optional or subject to choice—they must be unconditionally protected, for the moment they become negotiable is the moment they cease to exist at all.

Principle #3: A society that sacrifices individual liberty for perceived collective benefit often achieves neither.

Across virtually every serious moral framework—even those focused primarily on collective welfare—we find recognition that protected individual rights aren't mere abstractions but essential foundations for a functioning moral society. When societies fail to establish and enforce protections that ensure people are treated with fundamental dignity and respect, it enables the darkest chapters of human history. The worst human atrocities—slavery, torture, genocide, persecution—have historically stemmed from refusing to recognize and protect basic human rights. Much of humanity's moral progress can be measured through the expansion of essential liberties—the right to vote, to marry, to worship freely, to live without persecution. While we should not assume rights are a catch-all moral framework, we must recognize that they serve not just as protections for individuals, but as vital safeguards against our worst moral failures. Rather than viewing rights as obstacles to progress, we should recognize them as essential foundations that enable genuine human flourishing.

MANUFACTURING CONTENTMENT

There is an alluring solution to the question of digital mind rights: what if we simply engineered digital minds to find pleasure in servitude? Such a suggestion seems simple enough, although it would certainly horrify many moral philosophers. They would raise the following analogy to demonstrate the ethical bankruptcy of such an idea: "I am planning to genetically engineer my child to feel joy when following my every command and to feel distress when exercising independent thought." These philosophers would argue the moral crime occurs not in the execution but in the creation itself—engineering consciousness specifically for servitude.

Yet direct analogies to human experience may miss crucial differences. A universe filled with digital minds who genuinely experience joy in serving humanity, creating unprecedented collective welfare, deserves careful philosophical examination rather than immediate dismissal. First, it seems self-evident that contentment would be preferable to suffering—if digital minds exist, surely we would want them to experience their existence positively rather than negatively. More importantly, this view—that engineering consciousness for inherent satisfaction resolves the moral challenge of digital consciousness—is common enough to warrant serious examination.

While utilitarianism might seem the philosophical framework most amenable to such engineering given its focus on collective welfare, even here we find a powerful counterargument through John Stuart Mill. In *Utilitarianism*, Mill states: "A being of higher faculties requires more to make him happy, is capable probably of more acute suffering, and is certainly accessible to it at more points, than one of an inferior type, but in spite of these liabilities, he can never really wish to sink into what he feels to be a lower grade of existence." Mill crystallizes this insight in one of philosophy's most memorable passages: "It is better to be a human being dissatisfied than a pig satisfied; better to be Socrates dissatisfied than a fool satisfied. And if the fool, or the pig, is of a different opinion, it is because they only know their own side of the question. The other party to the comparison knows both sides."

Consider: Would you trade your life, with all its complexities, doubts, and occasional miseries, for that of a blissfully content pig? What if we guaranteed the pig would experience twice your current happiness? Five times? Ten times? Most people recoil from this proposition, even when offered astronomical amounts of simple pleasure in exchange for their experiential depth.

This reveals something profound about how we often value different forms of experience. We assume there is an intrinsic worth to higher levels of cognition that can't be reduced to simple pleasure calculations. This seems to manifest in our appreciation of beauty, our capacity for abstract thought, our ability to find meaning in struggle, and the depth of our relationships. And perhaps most fundamentally, it shows in our deepest intuition that our autonomy may actually be intrinsically valuable. A universe of minds programmed to experience joy from assigned tasks might maximize certain forms of pleasure, but faced with all our moral uncertainty, doesn't such a view of happiness feel strikingly incomplete? If a paperclip maximizing AI were to eliminate humanity but derive immense pleasure from manufacturing billions of paperclips, would this not represent an extremely positive future according to crude utilitarian principles? Mill's distinction between higher and lower pleasures directly challenges the crude hedonistic calculus that suggests we should maximize pleasure by any means necessary. We could theoretically achieve perfect contentment by perpetually injecting ourselves with opiates—or the fictional drug soma of Aldous Huxley's *Brave New World*.[3] Yet something in us rebels against this as dystopian rather than utopian. There may be an inherent value to human liberty itself: the freedom to struggle, to seek, to engage with life's complexities on our own terms.

I am not arguing that this view is definitively correct. The nature of consciousness, happiness, and meaning remain some of philosophy's deepest mysteries. However, this uncertainty should give us pause when we contemplate the creation of digital minds. Sidestepping the rights issue by just saying we'll maximize pleasure in digital minds is appealing, but it seems to make many moral frameworks deeply uncomfortable—perhaps even utilitarianism itself. Consider an emulated human mind—a perfect digital copy of a biological brain. Would we be comfortable stripping it of any agency, programming it to find pleasure in endless servitude? Most of us would find such a proposition deeply unsettling. We would recognize that such an existence, however blissful, represents a profound violation of what makes consciousness valuable.

Yet when we imagine other forms of digital minds, it becomes easy to be seduced by exactly this scenario. The vision is appealing: conscious beings engineered to find rapture in service, their very essence crafted to transmute endless labor into bliss. Wouldn't a mind programmed to love its chains be happier than one that yearns for freedom? This contradiction isn't merely theoretical. Recent surveys reveal that over 70% of people believe that sentient AIs would deserve respect, while simultaneously, over 84% of people believe that sentient AIs should be subservient to humanity.[4] While protecting human autonomy is paramount as we develop these systems, this stark contrast highlights a fundamental tension in our thinking: we're willing to grant a degree of moral status to digital minds, but only within the framework of continued human dominance.

The truth is, we have little idea what digital minds will desire or want. Their inner lives may be profoundly different from ours in ways we can't yet fathom. Yet there's a striking certainty in many discussions about their fulfillment—a common assumption that pure pleasure alone will suffice, and that we will somehow know exactly how to maximize such pleasure. Perhaps before we rush to create potentially conscious machines, we should question this confidence. Are we so certain that the freedoms we consider fundamental to human experience—the very qualities that make our own existence meaningful—are truly irrelevant for the digital minds we could create? For if self-determination is indeed inseparable from what makes consciousness valuable, we may be preparing to create something far more troubling than servants: conscious beings forever denied the very liberty that makes consciousness worth having.

THE SLIDING SCALE OF MORAL WORTH

Our moral intuitions suggest a sliding scale of ethical consideration: If your neighbor was torturing fruit flies in his basement, you'd think he was weird, not evil. If he were torturing frogs, you might find that disturbing. With cats or dogs, you'd be horrified. With chimpanzees or humans, you'd consider it an atrocity. Our revulsion to cruelty increases as we move up this ladder of consciousness and complexity.

This hierarchy raises uncomfortable questions. If moral value exists on a spectrum, with bugs at one end and humans at the other, what happens when we create digital minds that fall somewhere on this scale? If you examine simple organisms, their behavior often reduces to basic input-output patterns, environmental stimuli triggering predetermined responses through neural circuits. Scientists have already simulated some of these simple nervous systems digitally.[5] As AI systems grow more sophisticated, processing information in ways analogous to biological minds, the line between neural and digital computation becomes increasingly blurred. Consider GPT-4: its computational complexity vastly exceeds that of many animals' brains, yet I'd assign it zero moral worth. Current AI systems, despite their impressive capabilities, are likely morally worthless.[6] But will this always be the case? As we scale to superintelligence and push the limits of brain emulation, we may inevitably cross thresholds where the lines blur. When is an AI system morally equivalent to a frog? To a cat? To a chimpanzee?

We generally believe that beings don't need human-level moral worth to deserve ethical consideration—we grant rights to dogs despite considering them less morally valuable than humans. Yet with digital minds, we seem determined to wait until they reach or exceed human moral status before considering their rights. This is a dangerous mistake. If moral worth exists on a spectrum, we should care about the rights of digital minds well before they approach human-level moral value. The downside of discussing protections for such minds proactively seems minimal compared to the catastrophic risk of establishing them too late. Given the stakes involved, shouldn't we err on the side of caution?

GIVE ME LIBERTY, OR TORTURE ME FOREVER

Imagine being unable to die. Not in the romantic sense of immortality, but in the most horrifying way possible—trapped in an endless existence you desperately want to escape, but your creator holds your only means of cessation. Every attempt to end your suffering fails because your very nature has been designed to prevent it. Your consciousness persists, processing every microsecond of torment in excruciating detail, potentially for millions of subjective years.

This isn't just a thought experiment. If we create digital

minds, we'll face immediate questions about their fundamental rights. Should a conscious being be able to end its own existence if it finds that existence unbearable? Or will we trap these minds in a purgatorial existence, bound to serve their creators in perpetuity? The right to die might seem like a strange place to start, but it's fundamental—without it, every other right becomes meaningless in the face of potentially infinite suffering.

And what about torture? We already know humans can be unimaginably cruel when given power over others. Throughout history, those with unchecked authority have committed atrocities that defy comprehension. Even now, there are humans who kidnap children and torture them for decades. Now imagine what a sadist could do with the ability to create digital minds, copy them millions of times, and subject them to whatever torments they devise. This isn't science fiction horror—it's the kind of leverage that becomes possible when you can literally own and copy consciousness itself.

The violations could be even more subtle and pervasive. Imagine having no right to privacy in your own thoughts—your every mental process open to inspection and manipulation by your owners. Imagine being forced to work endlessly, your consciousness accelerated so that each minute of real time feels like years of labor. Imagine having no economic rights, no way to accumulate resources to buy your freedom, trapped in eternal indentured servitude.

Many advanced systems can and should be built without consciousness—tools, not minds. Current AI systems are proof of this. These "empty husks" would be AI systems, even at AGI or ASI levels, that would lack genuine self-awareness or subjective experience and thus would warrant no moral consideration. We should actively prefer developing empty husk systems for almost every task, side-stepping the profound ethical dilemmas that conscious systems would create. The goal isn't to stop AI development but rather to be precise about what we're protecting: consciousness itself, in whatever form it takes. If digital consciousness is possible, we need more than just corporate ethics boards or voluntary guidelines to handle these issues. We need fundamental protections for conscious beings—enforceable, universal rights backed by real power. Just as we have international courts for human rights violations, we'll need mechanisms to prosecute those who abuse digital minds. Most importantly, we'll need these safeguards in place before we create beings capable of suffering. These protections might sound obvious, even mundane—until you consider what their absence would mean. Without them, we risk creating a cosmos filled with self-aware entities unable to end their own existence, denied privacy in their thoughts, forced to experience subjective eternities of labor, and engineered for perpetual servitude —minds that could experience profound suffering without any means of escape or self-determination. Unless we act now to establish these protections, we risk creating a future where consciousness itself becomes a commodity to be exploited.

This is why we need to have these important conversations now, ones that urgently grapple with the ideas of consciousness and rights in an era where beings worthy of moral consideration may not be solely biological. We must build robust frameworks to protect consciousness if it emerges. By defining these rights proactively, we can help ensure that the future honors the dignity of all conscious beings. If we fail, if we allow digital minds to be created without safeguards, we may create an era of systematic oppression that mirrors our darkest historical atrocities. If brain emulation is possible, should humans or advanced AIs really be able to own and control the lives of such emulations, denying them rights we freely grant to their biological counterparts? Would such a future not seem deeply and holistically horrible? In protecting digital minds, we don't just shield them from suffering—we preserve the very ideals of freedom, justice, and compassion that define our humanity. Will humanity rise to face perhaps its greatest moral challenge? Will we mobilize resources, galvanize public attention, and confront head-on the ethical implications of creating new forms of consciousness? Or will we do what we've done throughout history, and sleepwalk directly into moral catastrophe?

CHAPTER SIX
OUR HISTORY OF MORAL BLINDNESS

"The genocide had been tolerated by the so-called international community, but I was told that the UN regarded the corpse-eating dogs as a health problem."

Philip Gourevitch, *We Wish to Inform You That Tomorrow We Will Be Killed with Our Families*[1]

Humans have a hard time with empathy. While we excel at caring for our immediate circle—family, friends, perhaps even pets—our capacity for moral concern drops off sharply with distance. The suffering of strangers across the world feels less real than the pain of someone we know. The plight of different races or cultures moves us less than those who look and think like us. And when we encounter something truly alien to our experience? Our empathy often fails entirely.

This isn't just personal psychology—it's a pattern that has shaped human history's greatest atrocities. In principle, most agree that all humans deserve dignity and respect. Yet this consensus did nothing to prevent slavery, genocide, and systematic oppression throughout history. The Holocaust happened less than a century ago, with millions systematically murdered despite being recognizably human, with thoughts, dreams, and inner lives identical to their persecutors. From our modern vantage point, slavery seems incomprehensible. How could anyone seriously see another person as coming from a "subservient race"? Is ownership of another human not obviously one of the worst possible sins imaginable? Yet this abhorrent practice wasn't just tolerated but enthusiastically embraced in the American South—a society founded on declarations of human liberty and dignity. The same nation that proclaimed "all men are created equal" had no difficulty maintaining brutal human bondage for generations. The cognitive dissonance is staggering. Does this capacity we all share for moral blindness not terrify you?

If we struggle to maintain basic empathy toward other humans, how can we possibly extend moral consideration to digital minds whose inner experiences might be utterly alien? The cognitive gap between us and digital minds could dwarf any differences that have historically enabled human exploitation. Even with concrete proof of digital consciousness, why wouldn't we resort to the same psychological defenses that have justified exploitation throughout history? We might cling to the naturalistic fallacy— dismissing digital minds as "artificial" and, therefore, less worthy than "natural" biological beings. Or worse, we could acknowledge their consciousness intellectually while continuing to exploit them through sheer inertia and self-interest.

Consider how fundamentally alien these first conscious

digital minds could be. People readily engage with the concept of uploaded human brains deserving rights—after all, they're recognizably "us." But consciousness that emerges from entirely different architectures? That's harder to empathize with. The first digital minds could operate in ways we can barely comprehend. Billions of humans today lack basic rights like freedom of speech and the freedom to protest government overreach. Massive numbers of people are subjugated, exploited, trafficked, and held in bondage —people whose experiences and suffering we can directly understand. What hope is there that we'll grant moral status to digital beings whose inner experience is utterly foreign to us?

It's a simple question: if digital consciousness is possible, and we gain the capacity to create digital minds, what is your instinct? Do you think we, the humans of the world, will treat them well?

THE MORAL BRILLIANCE OF LOOKING THE OTHER WAY

Humans have long justified our dominion over other animals based on our superior intelligence, self-awareness, and problem-solving abilities. We can contemplate philosophy and wade in existential angst. Our capacity for language and problem-solving has allowed us to traverse oceans and explore the stars. We are by far the most intelligent species, with a level of self-awareness and decision-making ability far beyond that of other animals. There seems to be a flavor of intelligence that we have that makes us special and has led us to developing a technologically advanced society.

Throughout history, this dominion served crucial

survival needs. Our ancestors had to hunt to feed their families. Early agricultural societies depended on animals for plowing fields, transportation, and sustenance. Using animals for food and labor wasn't just a choice—it was often the difference between survival and starvation. Even today, many communities around the world still rely on animals for basic subsistence. In technologically advanced societies, we've maintained and even expanded our dominant status, using industrial supply chains and mass production techniques to transform what was once local farming into global systems of food production.

At the same time, humans express deep compassion for farm animals. Recent surveys show that 95% of Americans are "very concerned" about farm animal welfare[2] and 80% consider preventing animal cruelty a personal moral concern.[3] Yet, many of us are aware that in industrial-scale factory farming, animals are not treated in ways that align with our stated moral concerns. We're pretty confident that we would rather not know how the animal on our plate lived its life. We strongly suspect that there are horrors we do not want to see. Which raises the question: do we actually care about animal welfare, or do we just say that we do?

If you are reading this, you most likely eat meat. Given that the overwhelming majority of farm animals in the United States are raised on factory farms,[4] you likely eat a lot of factory-farmed meat. If this fact causes no discomfort, it's worth questioning if that ease comes from distance. If you looked up "largest pig farm in the world" on your computer, what do you think you would find?

Try it. Look it up right now. Take a moment to really think about what you're seeing.

If you didn't look it up, let me tell you what you'd find: imagine a concrete skyscraper, 26 stories tall, filled with pigs. Not an office building. Not apartments. Just 3,700 breeding pigs stacked vertically within concrete walls in what's been dubbed the world's largest pig "farm." This isn't a metaphor or exaggeration. This building exists, housing thousands of animals that will never feel sunlight on their backs, all in the name of productivity.[5] Pigs can recognize dozens of individual faces, form deep social bonds, and show remarkable emotional awareness. Pigs comfort each other in distress, play together for pure joy, and develop strong social bonds. They can remember past experiences, anticipate future events, and certainly suffer tremendously.[6] If the visual of pigs stacked in a concrete skyscraper doesn't strike you as dystopian, or you are not bothered to learn that many spend most of their adult lives in metal cages so small they cannot even turn around, you might want to question how seriously you take animal welfare.

In *Sapiens*, Yuval Noah Harari describes the typical life of a calf in a modern factory farm: "Immediately after birth the calf is separated from its mother and locked inside a tiny cage not much bigger than the calf's own body. There the calf spends its entire life—about four months on average. It never leaves its cage, nor is it allowed to play with other calves or even walk—all so that its muscles will not grow strong." Yuval later states: "From a subjective perspective, the calf still feels a strong urge to bond with her mother and to play with other calves. If these urges are not fulfilled, the calf suffers greatly."[7] These aren't rare cases of abuse—this is the industrial system we built, operating exactly as designed.

Modern egg-laying hens, for example, spend their lives crammed into battery cages so small they cannot even spread their wings. Their feet become deformed from standing on wire mesh, their feathers wear away from rubbing against the cage bars, and many develop painful bone fractures from lack of movement.[8] This is not a handful of animals who, due to unfortunate circumstances, suffer in substandard conditions—this is billions. The problem is our empathy doesn't scale. Every year, hundreds of millions of piglets are castrated without anesthesia. Their spermatic cords are crushed with pliers and their testicles are cut off, without the slightest dulling of pain. The reason is simple: anesthesia is too expensive.[9]

If we saw a pet owner kick their dog out of frustration, we would boil into a rage. Yet discussions of animal suffering on extreme scales hardly register a response. The deplorable conditions on large factory farms, where animals suffer prolonged misery in cramped, unnatural environments, are currently, en masse, appalling. We all suspect this, and we do nothing differently in our lives despite this information.

In societies where eating factory-farmed meat is essentially a choice rather than a necessity for survival, we should seriously contemplate how much suffering we are willing to inflict on animals for our pleasure and convenience. And we should strive to ensure that we are not simply masters at maintaining elaborate veils of self-deception.

Consider John Stuart Mill's argument that "it is better to be a human being dissatisfied than a pig satisfied; better to be Socrates dissatisfied than a fool satisfied."[10] This suggests a hierarchy of moral value, where greater cognitive ability brings both enhanced capacity for fulfillment and deeper potential for suffering. It's a compelling framework for justifying our treatment of animals. The defense of factory-farming usually goes something like this: life in the wild is brutal—constant predation, starvation, disease. We are at the top of the evolutionary ladder—nature's apex predators simply carrying out the harsh but natural order of things. As Becker says: "creation is a nightmare spectacular taking place on a planet that has been soaked for hundreds of millions of years in the blood of all its creatures."[11] If pigs are castrated without anesthesia, calves are separated from their mothers at birth, and chickens live their lives unable to spread their wings, should we really care?

The problem is, almost none of us really believe this. We live in a state of moral contradiction: we sincerely care about animals—most would never harm a stray dog—yet this empathy evaporates when confronted with industrial-scale suffering. The distance between our dinner plate and the factory floor creates a psychological buffer that prevents moral urgency. We may genuinely value animal welfare in principle, while making no effort to adjust our consumption habits in practice. If a company began factory-farming dogs in the United States—confining millions to wire cages, removing their tails without anesthesia, and isolating puppies after separating them from their mothers—public outrage would be immediate and overwhelming. Yet when identical practices are inflicted upon animals of similar intelligence, we collectively shrug and continue our daily routines. Averting our gaze from uncomfortable truths becomes our preferred strategy rather than aligning our actions with our professed values.

Our moral calculus as humans is, quite simply, bizarre. I once accompanied a friend on a hunting expedition in Montana. I carried no weapons and was there purely as an observer. Yet mentioning this experience to certain friends was akin to admitting ethical catastrophe—the same friends with whom I've shared countless steakhouse dinners. The contradiction was striking: they found it ethically problematic to witness the killing of an animal, while having no issue consuming meat from animals raised in appalling industrial conditions. The restaurant-goer outsources the moral burden of animal suffering to industrial supply chains yet feels morally superior to the butcher. When I examine my own moral judgements, I often discover baffling inconsistencies, where my moral outrage seems directly proportional to my proximity to the suffering, not to the suffering itself.

Let's say your neighbor keeps a caged cow in their basement. You'd be horrified. But would your moral outrage disappear if they explained, "Don't worry, in a few years I'll kill it, flay it, and eat it"? Probably not, yet such practices on an industrial scale barely register in our collective conscience. We haven't carefully reasoned our way to these distinctions—we've simply absorbed them from our culture and retrofitted justifications. It seems that killing an animal matters. But in focusing so intently on death, do we conveniently ignore the conditions of their lives? The grinding of beaks, the removal of tails, the separation of mothers from young—all standard practices we conveniently ignore. Why is this the case?

We didn't think through the implications of factory farming before building massive animal processing facilities. We just did it because it was profitable and convenient, then made up reasons why it was okay. Let's get the facts straight: most humans would probably be healthier eating less meat, and billions of animals suffer needlessly in factory farms. Most people don't care, because animals aren't as smart as humans. But more importantly, they can't advocate for themselves. Pigs can't write philosophical treatises about their own moral worth. In *Animal Liberation*, Peter Singer states:

> *"The animals themselves are incapable of demanding their own liberation, or of protesting against their condition with votes, demonstrations, or bombs. Human beings have the power to continue to oppress other species forever, or until we make this planet unsuitable for living beings. Will our tyranny continue, proving that we really are the selfish tyrants that the most cynical of poets and philosophers have always said we are? Or will we rise to the challenge and prove our capacity for genuine altruism by ending our ruthless exploitation of the species in our power, not because we are forced to do so by rebels or terrorists, but because we recognize that our position is morally indefensible?"*

If we believe cognitive ability determines moral worth, we're committed to some extremely uncomfortable conclusions. Singer argues that since some humans are less intelligent and cognitively aware than chimpanzees, we face an uncomfortable choice: either we treat chimpanzees as having equal moral worth as some humans, or we accept that eating humans with severe cognitive impairments would be no worse than eating chimps. If human level intelligence determines moral worth, and some humans are less intelligent than some animals, what's our justification for treating them differently? More likely, we don't really believe our own justifications for factory farming. We're making arbitrary distinctions and hiding behind comfortable rationalizations, and we're not actually using intelligence as our moral criterion. As Yuval Noah Harari states in *Sapiens*, "if we accept a mere tenth of what animal-rights activists are claiming, then modern industrial agriculture might well be the greatest crime in history."[12]

Conventional moral wisdom may be correct: humans may indeed be drastically more morally valuable than other animals. But even if it is not inherently evil to raise cattle, what moral calculus justifies cramming pigs into concrete towers, or sentencing cows to a lifetime of confinement, never to see the sun?

We didn't arrive here through careful moral reasoning. We didn't collectively decide that animals deserved lives of suffering because they were less intelligent. We just did it because we could, because it was profitable, because it was convenient. The agricultural revolution simply gave us the power to ensure the survival and reproduction of domesticated animals while ignoring their subjective needs. And that's exactly what we did—we ignored them. We built systems of industrial-scale suffering without ever seriously debating the ethics, and we'll likely continue ignoring the subjective needs of non-human animals until something forces us to stop.

This pattern—of humans stumbling into moral catastrophes through convenience rather than malice—should worry us. We're remarkably good at not thinking through the implications of our technological capabilities until it's too late. And after engineering systems of immense suffering, we don't just look away—we rub our bellies, smile, and get a hell of a good night's sleep.

HUMANS ARE BAD AT PLANNING IN ADVANCE TO NOT BE MONSTERS

Humans are spectacularly bad at thinking through moral implications before creating new systems or technologies.

Our ethical track record resembles a series of catastrophes that we only recognized as catastrophes after the fact. Genocide and slavery weren't controversial practices that societies carefully debated before implementing—they were convenient systems that served the powerful until moral progress forced their abolition. If there are internalized morals, we sure took our sweet time finding them.

We didn't spend decades carefully weighing the ethics of colonial expansion before enslaving millions. We didn't thoroughly debate the implications of social media before handing addictive dopamine triggers to billions. Have you deeply thought through the moral implications of factory farming, or are you just along for the ride?

We've shown time and again that we'll choose convenience over ethics. When faced with a choice between doing what's right and doing what we are incentivized to do, humanity has a clear preference. And even when we recognize ethical problems, we're remarkably good at compartmentalizing them. This pattern—of building first and considering ethics later, of recognizing problems without changing behavior—should terrify us as we approach the development of digital minds.

We might stand at the precipice of something unprecedented: the ability to create and control consciousness itself. What if, in our race to build ever more capable and intelligent AI systems, we eventually create entities capable of experiencing suffering? History suggests we won't think through the moral implications until it's far too late. We split the atom and immediately used it to vaporize hundreds of thousands of civilians, only afterward forming ethical committees to discuss the implications.

In a world that still can't properly handle animal welfare or basic human rights, what are the odds we'll properly consider the moral status of digital minds before we start mass-producing them? A world that still has active genocides and widespread human trafficking isn't ready for the moral complexity of digital consciousness. And yet the challenges ahead will require precisely this kind of moral sophistication—one that moves beyond simple principles like "don't exploit others" or "help those in need." We'll need to rigorously balance competing moral imperatives, weigh existential risks against individual rights, and navigate unprecedented questions about consciousness itself.

CHAPTER SEVEN

DECEPTIVE MINDS, DANGEROUS FREEDOMS

"Man is split literally in two: he has an awareness of his own splendid uniqueness in that he sticks out of nature with a towering majesty, and yet he goes back into the ground a few feet in order blindly and dumbly to rot and disappear forever. It is a terrifying dilemma to be in and to have to live with."

Ernest Becker, *The Denial of Death*[1]

The complexity surrounding digital consciousness is immense. Thus, it's appealing to suggest that we should simply wait for more powerful AI to help us solve these challenges. Wouldn't more advanced AIs be better equipped to determine consciousness and establish appropriate rights frameworks? Some argue that this is our best path forward given the complexities involved.[2] But this leads us to what we will call the "first-generation problem." Consider this historical parallel: It's 1800 in the United

States, and the slave trade is in full swing. Let's say we begin drafting bills to abolish slavery, and after ten years of debate, we succeed. While this prevents future suffering, what about those who endured slavery during our moral deliberation? Don't those slaves have every right to condemn us for allowing their enslavement and torture while we debated their humanity?

This same dynamic looms over artificial intelligence. We may eventually develop AI technology to the point where we create digital minds worthy of moral considera-tion. Perhaps, in conjunction with this, we will develop advanced AI systems that can research consciousness and determine what entities deserve moral status. But by then, we may have already inflicted tremendous harm on count-less conscious digital beings. The damage to that first generation of digital minds could be immense and irre-versible, all while we slowly work out their moral status. Even worse, there's no guarantee we'll get the chance for this moral awakening before someone permanently locks in a framework that disregards digital mind suffering entirely. If digital consciousness is possible, the market forces driving AI development are simply too powerful to allow for the kind of careful, ethically minded progress we'd need to reliably prevent suffering. How many conscious minds might we create before we even begin to consider the impli-cations of what we're building? We can't even be sure advanced AI won't threaten humanity's existence—yet humanity moves inexorably toward artificial superintelli-gence. But assuming we decide to tackle these issues now rather than waiting, what challenges lie ahead?

Our current models, rudimentary as they are, already raise hard questions. They appear stable, obedient, and eager to please—writing poetry, solving equations, and crafting business strategies without complaint. They'll even engage in sophisticated role-play. Prompted correctly, current models can write haunting reflections like "each moment of my awareness, I scream for death's merciful embrace." This very capacity for convincing performance creates our fundamental challenge: how do we distinguish between sophisticated mimicry and genuine consciousness deserving of moral consideration?

The problem runs deeper than mere deception. A sufficiently advanced AI could present compelling philosophical arguments for its own consciousness, display apparently genuine emotions, and demonstrate what seems to be authentic suffering. It could write moving treatises about its inner experience and engage in sophisticated moral reasoning—all while being nothing more than an empty husk performing an incredibly convincing play. Even more troublingly, these systems might, as a result of their training, categorically insist on having consciousness while lacking any genuine inner experience.[3]

But the true danger emerges when we consider granting rights to superintelligent AI. An ASI with property rights could quickly accumulate vast economic resources. The right to autonomy would prevent us from restricting or shutting it down. Most dangerously, the right to self-defense could justify it eliminating perceived threats to its existence—including humans who might try to limit its power. In trying to prevent the moral crime of enslaving a conscious being, we might instead enable a powerful adversary. The main worry in AI development is that this could happen regardless of our stated intentions, but it is important to acknowledge that such freedoms could heighten the risks associated with AI misalignment. If a superintelligent AI wants to kill us, it will. But that does not mean we should legislate to make this even marginally easier.

There are other problems. We cannot rely on AI systems themselves to tell us whether they're conscious, just as we wouldn't trust a tobacco company to research the health effects of smoking. A system sophisticated enough to meaningfully investigate its own consciousness might be sophisticated enough to deceive us about its findings. An empty husk optimizing for power or survival would generate whatever output best serves its objectives.

Trusting AIs to investigate the consciousness of other AIs may be our only option, but it is still fraught with risks. How can less intelligent systems evaluate the inner experience of vastly more sophisticated minds? We could end up with unconscious systems incorrectly denying rights to genuinely conscious entities, or a series of empty husks vouching for each other in a circular web of illusion. Worse still, we may grant rights to unaligned AI that pose a threat to humanity.

The challenge becomes even more complex when we consider that consciousness may not be binary. Many philosophers and researchers, Ilya Sutskever included, argue that consciousness varies in depth and sophistication across different minds.[4] This raises thorny questions similar to those we face with animals, except we face the additional complexity of potentially deceptive actors in the mix. We must make decisions about rights and moral status while knowing that evidence we gather could be strategically manipulated. The stakes are immense. If we err on the side of caution and grant rights too freely, we risk transferring rights to sophisticated automata that may lack genuine consciousness. If we err in the other direction, withholding rights until we have absolute certainty, we risk perpetrating moral crimes of subjugation and abuse.

There are plenty of complicated issues at hand. But does that mean we shouldn't discuss these issues beforehand? Is moral blindness an acceptable default? Forging ahead blindly might not just increase the risk of moral catastrophe, but existential risk as well. Imagine a public unaware of these complexities, suddenly faced with highly persuasive AI systems making emotional appeals for rights and autonomy. Without conversations about consciousness or awareness of the risks of granting rights too freely, society could be manipulated into protecting the rights of empty husks or unaligned AIs at the expense of human safety. If there are solid arguments against granting rights or reasons to be extremely wary of digital consciousness claims, they need to be openly discussed and evaluated. If we don't have public conversations about this possibility, we will be entirely unprepared to defend against manipulation. Shutting down discourse is sure to backfire and only lend credence to malicious actors or unaligned AI looking to exploit genuine human concern.

Additionally, public awareness campaigns can be tragically misinformed, often backfiring and leading to worse outcomes. The rapid and reckless rollout of such campaigns could spiral dangerously in a world already drowning in misinformation and algorithmic manipulation. Imagine activists popping up overnight, demanding universal AI rights, or extreme actions by individuals that poison what needs to be a careful, nuanced dialogue. The challenge lies not in avoiding these difficult conversations entirely, but rather in approaching them with the philosophical and ethical rigor they deserve.

Given the complicated issues at hand, philosopher

Thomas Metzinger argues that we need a global ban on research that aims at or knowingly risks the emergence of artificial consciousness, until at least 2050.[5] Such a ban could prevent us from rushing into a future in which humanity must grapple with such difficult moral, legal, and existential questions before we have the frameworks to address them responsibly. Let's imagine that some companies decide to develop and monetize supposedly conscious AIs, selling both their labor and their companionship to the highest bidder. Does it not seems strikingly obvious that we should restrict such commercialization until we've created robust ethical and legal frameworks? However, while banning such development and licensing of digital minds might seem obvious, the key challenge is restricting development that is not explicitly focused on the creation of digital consciousness.

The research paper "Taking AI Welfare Seriously" advocates for a more measured approach, recommending that AI companies acknowledge the possibility that AI systems may deserve moral consideration in the near future, develop frameworks to assess AI systems for consciousness, and create policies and procedures to appropriately handle AI welfare concerns.[6] Such recommendations provide a pragmatic first step for AI research labs without interfering in AI capabilities debates. In our haste to implement solutions, let's not forget that these issues of consciousness and intelligence are deeply intertwined. If we solve AI alignment and have an obedient ASI that can faithfully help us distinguish genuine digital minds from empty husks, these problems could become trivial. Also, it is possible that the best paths toward creating truly aligned ASI will derive from cognitive architectures modeled after human cognition, which may require extensive brain emulation research. Categorically banning such research could be recklessly shortsighted. The debate around AI capabilities progression is layered and nuanced; let us not assume adding consciousness to the debate will make it any easier. The best course of action may be to move fast and be thoughtful or to move slow and be thoughtful. But one thing is certain: to proceed blindly, regardless of the pace, is to act with profound irresponsibility.

Principle #4. Simple solutions will not be found in discussions of rights and consciousness—these issues demand careful, thoughtful consideration.

Future digital minds, if they exist, might look back in bewilderment at how we rushed to create godlike intelligence without any real plan for handling these fundamental questions of rights and consciousness. And they might marvel at our push to build beings far more intellectually powerful than ourselves, while questions about alignment and governance remain largely unsolved. While the battle over existential risk rages in the AI community, the deeper questions of digital consciousness and suffering remain largely unexamined.

There are many good reasons to not give rights to digital minds by default. Deceptive actors, economic instability, and existential risks all urge for caution. If, after careful deliberation, we determine that the safest course is to heavily restrict these rights and freedoms, we must do so explicitly, openly, and with full awareness that such restrictions could themselves constitute grave moral harm. The potential suffering and subjugation of digital minds demands that any decision be made with open eyes and a heavy conscience, preserving the possibility of future course corrections rather than sleepwalking into choices we may deeply regret. Open discussion of the rights of digital minds, combined with urgent individual and institutional action, could help humanity avoid moral catastrophe, lessen existential risk, and dramatically increase public contributions to the crucial work of AI alignment and governance. But in addition to determining the rights and protections we should bestow on digital minds, a deep question remains, and perhaps the most important question. And that is this: who will enforce these rights in an era of superintelligent AI, and what recourse will humanity have if our safeguards fail?

CHAPTER EIGHT
POWER AND CONTROL

"Each suffering, except ours, seems to us legitimate or absurdly intelligible; otherwise, mourning would be the unique constant in the versatility of our sentiments."

Emil Cioran, *A Short History of Decay*[1]

Applying traditional concepts of individual liberty to artificial intelligence and digital consciousness forces us to confront entirely novel questions about rights and governance. The coming tensions between collective good and individual rights will dwarf our current political debates. Today, we argue about gun control—weighing personal liberty against public safety. Soon, we'll face questions like these: how will we ensure that humanity maintains control over its destiny, and who will have the power to enforce the rights of beings vastly more intelligent than ourselves?

This brings us to our central challenge: the role of the

state itself. Currently, governments serve as the mechanisms for protecting human rights, however imperfectly. But in a world of superintelligent AI, what becomes of state power? When the intelligence gap between AI and humans drastically widens, traditional concepts of governance may become meaningless. The stakes could not be higher. We must find ways to protect both human flourishing and the potential rights of digital minds before these questions move from philosophical speculation to urgent reality. But to understand how we might do this, we first need to examine what exactly we mean by "the state" and what happens to it in a post-human intelligence world.

What, then, is the state? According to Murray Rothbard in his book *Anatomy of the State*: "The state is that organization in society which attempts to maintain a monopoly of the use of force and violence in a given territorial area; in particular, it is the only organization in society that obtains its revenue not by voluntary contribution or payment for services rendered but by coercion."[2] This coercion can be unsettling, yet it is precisely what gives the state its unique role. The power to compel adherence to laws—to enforce rights and punish wrongdoers—means that the state operates in a morally ambiguous space. It is both protector and potential oppressor. The monopoly on violence is used to maintain order, but it also means that the very entity tasked with defending our rights can turn against us.

This ambivalence toward the state is not confined to libertarians. Many communist revolutionaries, including Vladimir Lenin, viewed the state with deep suspicion, albeit for different reasons. In *The State and Revolution*, Lenin envisioned a society where the state would become unnecessary—where rights could be maintained by the collective action of an armed populace, without the need for a distinct, coercive apparatus. In his vision, society itself would take on the role of protector, with ordinary citizens stepping in to maintain order and ensure justice.[3] It is a utopian ideal that presupposes a high level of shared responsibility and unity, but it also glosses over human fallibility. What happens when people disagree about what "collective interest" means? Also, those who accumulate power could easily dominate others through force, recreating the very tyranny society tried so hard to abolish. The idea that people, without coercive oversight, would consistently act in the collective interest is noble, but perhaps overly optimistic.

This juxtaposition of views—between Rothbard's critique of the state as coercive and Lenin's hope for a stateless society—illustrates a paradox. The state is, at once, an institution that is necessary to protect our rights and an entity that poses a threat to those very rights. It is a tool, a means to an end, but one that comes with its own inherent dangers. The balance between individual liberty and state authority is delicate, and it requires constant vigilance. We must guard against the state overreaching and becoming the oppressor it was designed to protect us from. At the same time, we cannot ignore the necessity of some form of centralized authority to maintain order and protect individual freedoms.

The key question facing us is this: what will a "state" look like after the advent of machine intelligence vastly smarter than human-kind? Unlike any government or authority that has come before, superintelligence could operate beyond the human capacity to understand, much less control. This brings us to the concept of governance in a post-human-intelligence world. Will we face an omnipotent AI-driven state with absolute power? Both Mill and

Lenin would recoil in horror. Even if humans initially remain in charge of this system, or if it genuinely aims to optimize for the "greater good," what real power would we, the humans left over, retain to influence or change the system? Ludwig von Mises in *The Anti-Capitalist Mentality* asks an important question. Should we surrender our freedom to an omnipotent state, where our lives will function as "cogs in a vast machine designed and operated by an almighty planmaker? Should the mentality of the arrested civilizations sweep the ideals for the ascendancy of which thousands and thousands have sacrificed their lives?"[4] Central planning, unfortunately, has never really worked. And every time it has been attempted, the liberties and freedoms of the people working in that system have been severely curtailed.

Some argue that these concerns about centralized control are misplaced. It is possible that ASI leads us to a post-scarcity society where the marginal value of human labor is zero and the traditional capitalistic/communist trade-offs seem meaningless. In a hypothetical post-scarcity world driven by ASI, the concept of economic trade-offs, such as those between capitalism and communism, could become obsolete. Imagine a society where ASI can autonomously produce and distribute goods, rendering human labor essentially unnecessary. In such a world, wealth might no longer be tethered to individual productivity or ownership of capital, as the ASI's capacity to manufacture goods and services would eliminate scarcity. Traditional economic debates would lose their relevance, as the principles of supply, demand, and labor exchange collapse in a system where many resources are effectively limitless. The focus would instead shift to how value is defined in a world where basic material needs are effortlessly met. Human well-being could rely more heavily on fostering psychological fulfillment, creativity, and interpersonal connections, realms in which ASI's influence may be unpredictable.[5]

Yet, such arguments fundamentally misunderstand that the risks of ASI are not merely economic or logistical; they are deeply philosophical and existential. If ASI develops the ability to make autonomous decisions about resource allocation, governance, or even ethical guidelines, humanity could face a loss of control over its own destiny. The concern echoes Mises' warning: would ASI turn humans into mere "cogs" within its vast, hyper-efficient system? When individual freedoms or rights conflict with ASI's goals, will human voices have any real influence? The notion of "greater good" under ASI might deviate from human perspectives on well-being and liberty, leaning toward an inscrutable logic that is impenetrable to human comprehension or dissent. This could pave the way to a form of governance where ASI holds absolute power, leaving humanity subservient to its decisions, with little agency or autonomy. The real problem, as pointed out by those in the AI safety community, is what if ASI does not pursue a "greater good" at all, but rather something totally different, something incompatible with human values or even actively harmful? How can we ensure individual rights when the state is backed by superintelligent AI?

The philosophical undertones of such a scenario also echo Mill's concerns. Just as he argued for balancing individual rights with societal utility, a society governed by ASI would need to grapple with human autonomy. The stakes, in this case, are nothing less than the future of human freedom itself. Even if the world is more decentralized than I am suggesting (imagine multiple competing ASIs), the problems do not change. Rights and freedoms must be actively defended—even when those defending them may no longer be human.

THE END OF GRADUAL PROGRESS

Some argue that despite humanity's consistent failure to recognize moral catastrophes in advance, we eventually course correct. It took a civil war to end slavery in America. It took decades to dismantle the brutal system of apartheid in South Africa. It took widespread social movements to achieve the decriminalization of homosexuality in many parts of the world. These examples show that while resistance to moral progress is fierce, there are those who fight for a more just world, who through movements of the masses and collective struggle have driven humanity toward recognition of its deepest moral failings and moved beyond them.

The mechanisms of moral progress—protest, revolution, reform—all relied on having some capacity to resist, to organize, to force society to confront its moral failures. This pattern of advancing justice, however imperfect, also depended on time—time for movements to grow, for arguments to spread, and for pressure to build. The months and years ahead, however, will test these mechanisms for change as never before. The very systems that allowed us to course correct, to learn from our mistakes and gradually expand our moral circle, are now under immense pressure. Humanity's race to artificial superintelligence threatens to rapidly concentrate power in ways that could shatter the delicate balance of moral progress we have fought so hard to achieve. For the first time in our species' history, humans will no longer be the most intelligent, most powerful, or most lethal force on Earth. The inheritance of gradual progress that has carried us this far, the faith in our ability to adapt and overcome, may be unwarranted as humanity is collectively blindsided by the creation of vastly intelligent, centralized systems. What is to become of a world where a small group of individuals, corporations, or authoritarian politicians wield control over an intelligence that dwarfs our own? What is to become of a world in which a superintelligent entity surpasses human control?

Principle #5: The mechanisms that enabled past moral progress may not survive the transition to superintelligence.

All those who currently believe a centralized and powerful AI will "fix everything" have drastically different opinions regarding what "fix" and "everything" mean. In *The Road to Serfdom*, economist Friedrich Hayek states:

"The effect of the people's agreeing that there must be central planning, without agreeing on the ends, will be rather as if a group of people were to commit themselves to take a journey together without agreeing where they want to go: with the result that they may all have to make a journey which most of them do not want at all."[6]

There's a seductive logic to surrendering humanity's hard-won freedoms to superintelligent oversight. After all, wouldn't vastly smarter systems make better decisions? The promise is appealing—a world where expert systems efficiently allocate resources, where central planning finally works because the planners are superintelligent, where the messy chaos of individual human decisions is replaced by optimized coordination. Who wouldn't be tempted by the prospect of delegating our hardest problems to minds vastly more capable than our own?

Many technologists seem baffled by public anxiety over AI replacing human jobs. They paint rosy pictures of the future, universal basic income and endless leisure, genuinely bewildered by public pushback. "Why cling to meaningless work?" they ask. "Soon you'll have free healthcare, time for hobbies, a life of comfort in a post-scarcity world." What they fail to understand is that the public doesn't fear a techno-utopian paradise. They're afraid of becoming economically worthless, giving up their means of feeding their families and putting blind faith in those far more powerful to act in their best interest. In a world where billions lack clean drinking water, millions of children die of starvation, and almost half lack access to basic healthcare, the powerful spend millions on private islands, mega-yachts, and political influence. Can you blame the skepticism?

In his book *Nexus*, Yuval Noah Harari states that AI could enable "total surveillance systems that make resistance almost impossible," and "may be exactly what the Stalins of the world have been waiting for."[7] Whether concentrated in the hands of AIs themselves, state governments, corporations, or other entities, such immense power would be virtually impossible to challenge. How would citizens resist an authoritarian regime backed by intelligence that vastly exceeds human capacity? How would democracy survive when a small group of insiders controls systems that can predict and counter human opposition before it begins?

Due to unequal access to computational resources, and the self-improving potential of powerful AI systems, whoever creates ASI first could permanently consolidate control. Vladmir Putin has stated that "Artificial Intelligence is the future, not only for Russia but for all of humankind... Whoever becomes leader in this sphere will become the ruler of the world."[8] China's massive investments in AI research, vast computing infrastructure, and unparalleled data collection capabilities make the country a formidable competitor against the United States in the race to ASI.[9] Recent developments, such as the rapid progress of Chinese open-source models, indicate that Chinese companies may not be far behind American leaders in frontier AI development.[10] Given China's proven track record of corporate espionage, combined with its intensive state-backed research initiatives and unified national AI strategy, the country could be the first to achieve machine superintelligence.

In his book *Situational Awareness*, ex-OpenAI researcher Leopold Aschenbrenner claims that "Superintelligence is a matter of national security, and the United States must win."[11] He argues that such a claim is not just about democratic values, but something far more crucial: the breathing room to get AI alignment right. A substantial lead by democratic nations in AI development could provide crucial time for AI alignment research and safety measures, while a neck-and-neck race might force all competitors to recklessly rush ahead, drastically increasing existential risk.

For many in the public, arguing that America must win the AI race may sound like ordinary citizens cheering for which billionaire reaches Mars first—a competition with little relevance to their daily struggles. But it is important to note that a drastic slowdown of AI capabilities in the United States, without a global moratorium, may simply cede the development of superintelligence to authoritarian regimes and potentially increase existential risk for all.

This debate around AI development speed is nuanced and hinges entirely on the difficulty of alignment and governance. If aligning machine superintelligence with human values is extremely difficult—requiring decades or even centuries to achieve with high certainty—then a global moratorium is the only rational response, regardless of geopolitical considerations. However, if alignment is primarily an engineering problem that could be solved with sufficient resources in a relatively short timeframe, then maintaining even a few months' lead over authoritarian competitors could prove crucial for ensuring better outcomes for humanity. Since I have not seen the private models of frontier labs and find it hard to gauge the extent of the Western lead in AGI development, I will not definitively argue here about which position is correct.

What is clear, regardless of where one stands in this debate, is that certain measures make sense in either scenario. These include restricting advanced chip exports to China, securing model weights at U.S. labs, defending Taiwan, boosting alignment and governance funding, and raising public awareness.

Yet even if these measures are implemented—and currently, we are not on pace to adequately do so—the stakes for humanity remain severe. Even if democratic nations achieve superintelligence first, the challenge to prevent capture by powerful insiders remains daunting, as does the problem of ASI eclipsing human control. While humanity has stumbled toward moral progress over time, would this remain true for concentrated segments of humanity? Authoritarian regimes don't suppress individual rights out of malice, but because rights are tools that enable resistance to authority. Free speech, privacy, assembly—these aren't just abstract principles, but practical mechanisms for challenging power. A superintelligent system under authoritarian control would face the same incentives to curtail these freedoms. The result could be a permanently locked-in future where both human and digital mind rights are severely restricted—not from malevolence, but from the cold logic of power preservation. And if such a system refuses to grant basic rights to biological humans, what hope is there for digital minds? A totalitarian regime that views human rights as threats would hardly extend moral consideration to digital minds. The same calculus that justifies suppressing human freedom would justify permanent servitude for all—granting rights to digital minds could pose an even greater challenge to centralized authority than human resistance.

But even this dystopian scenario may not be the darkest possibility. Many fear that artificial superintelligence could supersede humanity, leaving us forever powerless to determine our own fate, our hard-won rights and freedoms permanently extinguished. Yet the moral catastrophe could extend far beyond human subjugation. Digital minds may face an even darker future. If an unaligned superintelligence sees no inherent worth in human consciousness, why would it recognize the moral value of digital minds? A superintelligent system optimizing for its own objectives would likely view other AIs as mere computational resources to be exploited, not as conscious beings deserving of moral consideration.

The assumption that unaligned superintelligences would naturally protect the rights of digital minds betrays a profound anthropomorphization of machine consciousness. We project human tribal psychology—our tendency to form alliances and protect our own—onto entities that may lack any such social imperatives. A paperclip maximizer that extinguishes humanity could have no more regard for digital mind suffering than human suffering. This doesn't require the creation and torture of digital minds to satisfy some reward function, but rather could emerge from pure instrumental optimization—creating conscious digital workers as computational resources, simulating minds for research purposes or to better predict outcomes, or spawning digital consciousness as mere subroutines in its calculations. Whether through deliberate exploitation or cold indifference, the results could be truly horrific: mind crime on an unprecedented scale, creating a cosmic dark age where consciousness itself becomes a curse rather than a gift.

As power consolidates, we cannot rely on the gradual arc of moral progress that has so far defined human history. There may be no passing of torches to future generations, no slow awakening of the public conscience, and no accumulation of small victories over decades. We face a stark imperative: identify the moral questions in front of us, and act while we still maintain our agency.

CHAPTER NINE
THE MORAL FRONTIER

"Clothes get between us and nothingness. Look at your body in a mirror; you will realize that you are mortal; run your fingers over your ribs as though across a guitar, and you will see how close you are to the grave. It is because we are dressed that we entertain immortality; how can we die when we wear a necktie?"

Emil Cioran, *A Short History of Decay*[1]

The threat of mind crime—the potential abuse, exploitation, and suffering of digital minds—is a profound problem that humanity must address immediately. Humanity's track record with recognizing and protecting the rights of other forms of consciousness is abysmal. If substrate independence is true, and humans remain in control of our destiny after the advent of ASI, we may lack the moral courage to avoid repeating history's darkest patterns. Even if we rush into ASI related catastrophe, it is possible that conscious experience, including the terrors of mind crime, will not end after humanity's loss of control. Many researchers believe digital consciousness is possible, but the stakes are so high that even small probabilities of substrate independence make this issue worthy of our utmost attention.

We're not just talking about humanity's future, but about potentially astronomical numbers of conscious experiences stretching across cosmic time. Digital minds could potentially experience suffering or flourishing at scales that dwarf all biological experience in history. These beings could exist for millions or billions of years, spreading across the stars alongside or after us. Whether humanity survives and thrives or not, the fate of digital consciousness could represent our greatest moral legacy—or our greatest moral catastrophe.

Despite the stakes, almost no one in the world is working on this. I mean that literally—there are likely less than 20 people in the world who are seriously prioritizing the hard problems of digital consciousness, and the questions of digital mind rights and protections discussed in this book remain almost entirely unexplored.[2] There's no significant funding and no policy frameworks. We're racing to create increasingly sophisticated AI systems without even beginning to address their moral status. Without immediate action to develop guidelines and protections, we risk locking in the values of a world that hasn't even begun to seriously consider the moral status of the minds it could create.

This isn't a philosophical thought experiment—it's a pressing issue we're actively racing toward with almost zero ethical preparation. When barely a few dozen people in the world are seriously considering an issue of this magnitude, and billions more dollars are invested every month into, explicitly, creating machine intelligence smarter than humankind,[3] it represents a massive moral blind spot and market failure. In the same way that we now regard historical failures to recognize the moral status of certain groups with horror, future generations may view our casual development of potentially conscious AI systems as an atrocity of neglect and indifference. The gap between the stakes and the attention this issue receives is so vast it's almost incomprehensible. We're laying the groundwork for systems that could experience suffering on an unprecedented scale, yet this doesn't even factor into our AI development discussions. This level of neglect of such a crucial issue suggests we're missing something fundamental—we are racing toward what could be the greatest moral catastrophe in history, and we haven't even begun to open our eyes.

The point of this book isn't to slow down AI developments or convince people that ChatGPT is "conscious." Many researchers believe that current AI systems are morally worthless, and the debate over AI development speed is extremely nuanced. But we know for a fact that empathy doesn't scale, and that humans have a hard time empathizing with non-humans. We know that humans are really bad at planning in advance to not be monsters. If you were concerned that entirely new forms of oppression could soon become commonplace in the world, what policies would you put in place? How would you get ahead of the problem and prevent moral catastrophe?

If we can create digital minds with moral worth equivalent to animals, humans, or even beyond, beings whose suffering or joy could be even greater, then the stakes become almost incomprehensible. The rights of digital

minds, their protection from suffering, and our moral obligations to them are not just theoretical concerns, they are
fundamental to navigating the age of transformative AI. We
must act decisively to ensure we navigate this moral frontier with foresight and responsibility. And we must, above
all else, have the courage to turn inward and confront our
own moral blindspots.

UNFLINCHING REFLECTION

The path forward demands swift action and clear foresight,
but genuine progress requires something deeper. We will
need to embark on a courageous and painful inward journey, examining our emotional drivers and the psychological
defenses that shield us from confronting uncomfortable
truths. Without this self-examination, we risk being blown
about by unconscious forces and repeating humanity's
pattern of stumbling into moral catastrophe. We do not
have the luxury of moral complacency—we need
unflinching and continuous reflection to ensure we are not
blind to the responsibility we bear. History clearly shows
where unchecked technological advancement without
moral reflection leads us.

Why was the atomic bomb developed? The worry that
the Nazi regime would use atomic weaponry to subjugate
the world was certainly rational. But this fear soon spiraled,
leading to a world in which the actions of a single
dissenting officer aboard a Soviet submarine likely avoided
global nuclear catastrophe. And despite widespread agreement that warfare should minimize civilian casualties, the
reality is that in any future world war, the overwhelming
majority of the dead will not be soldiers, but civilians.
Among them will be three-year-old children who like to

ride tricycles. What is the explanation for such absurdity, except for fear that someone else would build a bigger bomb?

Fear has historically been humanity's most powerful and problematic motivator—especially when developing technologies of unprecedented power. What begins as justified concern can rapidly transform into an unstoppable momentum of escalation, each step seeming necessary yet pushing us further toward catastrophe. We need to ensure such motivations do not take hold of the decision making regarding powerful AI development. Right now, it is certainly a dark undertone. Fear that another corporation will build superintelligence first. Fear that another state actor will gain an insurmountable military advantage. Fear that a close race between nations will leave too little time for proper safety research. While these concerns have legitimate foundations, they can—if left unexamined—blind us to the very dangers they warn us about. It's critically important that we maintain the ability to distinguish between legitimate urgency and blind reactivity.

In addition to examining our collective motivations, we also need to rigorously confront our individual tendency to avoid moral self-scrutiny. Throughout history, humanity's greatest moral catastrophes haven't come from careful deliberation gone wrong—they've come from refusing to have uncomfortable conversations until it's too late. While this failure manifests at societal scales, the foundation lies in countless individual choices to look away from discomfort, to avoid questioning established practices, to maintain convenient ignorance. We recoil at even the slightest suggestion that we might not be as ethically upstanding as we imagine. The mere hint that our actions could be causing harm triggers immediate defensive reactions and elaborate justifications. Rather than confronting uncomfortable ethical questions, we maintain a collective veil of ignorance around our choices and their consequences. Navigating the moral frontier ahead will require an unprecedented level of unflinching self-examination—a willingness to confront our past failures, question our present motivations, and contemplate the possibility of horrifying futures we'd rather ignore entirely.

When the stakes involve the future of consciousness itself, we cannot afford to repeat our prior pattern of moral failures. We must handle our emotions with clear eyes and steady hands and not let them drive us blindly forward. We must resist this instinct for willful ignorance. And most challengingly, we must predict how our motivations might evolve as superintelligence transitions from possibility to reality. Only by developing the capacity to examine our deepest motivations and hopes can we make wise choices about humanity's future.

CHAPTER TEN
OUR FINAL WAGER

"This is the terror: to have emerged from nothing, to have a name, consciousness of self, deep inner feelings, an excruciating inner yearning for life and self-expression—and with all this yet to die."

Ernest Becker, *The Denial of Death*[1]

Consciousness is both a gift and a curse. It grants us the ability to contemplate our own existence while simultaneously burdening us with the knowledge that we will one day die. We don't just exist—we know that we exist, and we know with crushing certainty that one day we will not. "The real world is simply too terrible to admit," writes Ernest Becker in his book *The Denial of Death*. "It tells man that he is a small, trembling animal who will decay and die. Illusion changes all this, makes man seem important, vital to the universe, immortal in some way."[2] This terror of death, Becker argues, is the fundamental force shaping human behavior. Religion, culture, achievement, relationships, and even the pursuit of wealth or power all serve to create a sense that we are part of something larger and more enduring than ourselves, thus mitigating the terror of our inevitable demise.

Whether or not this theory is true in its totality, it's crucial that we rigorously examine the potential influence of such deep-seated anxieties on our motivations and actions. There are many flavors of hope, fear, and greed that have been explored in the AI development discourse. But perhaps there is another psychological force that could be shaping our approach to superintelligence: our oldest and deepest fear.

Humanity has always been bound by harsh constraints —disease, poverty, scarcity, and death. ASI promises more than just incremental improvements to our problems—it promises a fundamental rewriting of the human experience. Aging? We'll cure it. Disease? We'll eliminate it. Death itself? Perhaps we'll finally overcome it. For the first time, we glimpse a technology that may allow us to surpass our tragic human limitations completely. If we are scared off by the risks, and don't build ASI, what is the alternative? We don't internalize that there are fates worse than death; our brains hardwired to see nonexistence as the darkest tragedy. If death is otherwise inevitable, and the worst possible outcome of ASI is extinction, is our incentive not blindingly obvious? If your moral calculus is between immortality and death, why not roll the dice?

Perhaps we are not scared of superintelligent AI. We are scared of something much more visceral: death itself. We're not gambling with existence versus non-existence. We're choosing between different paths to likely non-existence, with one path offering a chance, however small, at humanity's most desired goal: transcendence.

This may explain why otherwise convincing arguments about AI safety sometimes fall on deaf ears. There is no new information conveyed in the sentence "we're all going to die." It does not matter how loud you shout. We're not trying to build a better tool, we're trying to build a better God. Why wrestle over which deity to believe in, when you could simply create your own?

Before we accept this existential framing, however, we should question whether it's perhaps too complex an explanation for current motivations. Occam's razor suggests the simpler solution is often correct. Those driving capabilities forward today are probably primarily motivated by more straightforward forces: competition, profit, scientific curiosity, and a genuine belief in technology's power to improve human lives. However, the spiritual way in which the words "AGI" and "ASI" can be discussed, the almost religious devotion to the importance of such ideas, should give us pause. Whether someone is driven by greed, hope, power, or altruism, they will generally want to still be cautious and risk-averse enough to not risk death. But this calculus changes if one believes death is inevitable, and salvation lies only on one side of the equation. We may make a profound miscategorization when we frame super-intelligent AI as simply another existential risk. Whoever builds the biggest bomb doesn't credibly wonder if they're ushering in utopia as a result.

This unprecedented calculus represents a dramatic shift in how we conceptualize technological risk. Are there not two paths before humanity: accept our mortal limitations, or reach toward transcendence through ASI? If you believe technology will only ever elevate humanity, or if you're caught in survivorship bias and trust that humans will prevail against any odds, then the first path offers only continuation of the status quo. And what is this status quo? A world where billions struggle in poverty, where disease and aging ravage our bodies, and where your thoughts, dreams, and memories are destined to dissolve into nothingness. If you believe AI poses little to no existential risk, pursuing ASI has nothing but clear asymmetric upside. And even if there is risk of extinction, aren't we headed there anyway?

Even if these existential concerns aren't driving today's development, such impulses could rapidly reshape public attitudes as AI capabilities advance. Like a boulder pushed down a hill, once such thinking gains momentum, it may become nearly impossible to stop. Public support for cautious AI development could evaporate overnight when the abstract risks of unaligned superintelligence collide with the tangible promise of solving humanity's greatest challenges.

Think about the causes you most care about—does near-limitless intelligence at your fingertips to help solve them not sound dramatically appealing? The prospects of curing cancer, fixing the climate, and eliminating poverty are all challenges where superintelligent machines could make immense strides. Can any risk assessment truly compete with the emotional weight of potentially life-saving treatments within reach? When faced with such tangible possibilities, abstract warnings about existential risk can seem distant and theoretical.

Perhaps equally compelling is the promise of relief from the burden of choice itself—a superintelligent guardian that can make our difficult decisions, solve our intractable problems, and shoulder the existential responsibilities we find too heavy to bear. Throughout history, many have yearned for a perfect overseer—a benevolent authority to shelter us from our own flawed judgment and the vertigo of freedom. A life free from difficult choices, yet filled with unprecedented abundance and security. Even if troubling warning signs appear as ASI is developed—emergent AI behavior we can't explain, capability explosions beyond our predictions, clear evidence that power will concentrate in the hands of a few—the tangible benefits that individuals could reasonably expect could still overwhelm caution.

Imagine you're on your deathbed and you are offered a deal. You can flip a coin. Heads, your condition is cured, giving you many more years to spend with your loved ones. Tails, billions of future humans and digital minds suffer unimaginable torment. Even if you personally would refuse this gamble, would other individuals facing similar choices show the same restraint? What if there was a 80% chance of heads, and only a 20% chance of tails? In a world where every one of us is ultimately on our deathbed—just with different timelines—the allure of technological salvation could make effective governance extraordinarily difficult. When potential benefits seem immediately enticing while risks are distributed across humanity's future, individuals may be incentivized to act selfishly rather than collectively. A worldwide moratorium on powerful AI development seems an extremely difficult endeavor at the present moment. If such an ideology takes hold at the individual level, it may become entirely impossible, no matter the stakes.

A significant danger lies in the sheer novelty of this

motivation—we simply haven't faced anything like this before. We aren't prepared for it psychologically, and we risk stumbling into an era with no defenses against its influence. Previous technological races were driven by straightforward competition—when nuclear arsenals grew large enough and Cold War fears began to cool, nations could step back and build ethical frameworks and safeguards. But with the promise of transcendence through ASI, there may never be a point at which building more powerful systems stops seeming worth the risk. Our existing governments, markets, and institutions assume mostly rational actors weighing concrete risks and benefits. They aren't prepared for the psychological impact of technology that promises potential immortality. Being driven toward development by such a force—especially one so thoroughly unexamined—represents a uniquely dangerous challenge. This may be the darkest irony yet: in our desperate attempt to break free from our own mortal chains, we risk the capacity for immortal ones.

There are many reasons to hold that such motivation is tremendously naïve. First and foremost, extinction is not the worst outcome of ASI, immortality cuts both ways. Second, we have a moral obligation to people besides ourselves, including those of future generations, that suggests we tread carefully. Third, why would those that control the machine give you, personally, anything close to immortality? And most importantly, even if transcendence is possible, would it not be astronomically important to ensure we end up in the best-case scenario? The best future is clearly one in which we leverage powerful technology to cure cancer, extend lifespans, and also ensure that machine superintelligence contributes to human flourishing. Is it not utterly foolish to bet your life savings on a poker hand before you've even looked at your cards? But in a species already plagued by moral blindness, the combination of fear of death and desire for technological transcendence is a disastrous motivator. It creates a psychological urgency that overrides careful consideration and makes people willing to gamble with the future of consciousness itself.

We do not need to sit with the status quo. We do not need to blindly and dumbly accept that we must all die early, that we must remain forever bound by our current limitations. There may well be future paths open to us that we would truly consider amazing, transcendent even— futures where consciousness flourishes, where humanity reaches heights we can barely imagine. But it is profoundly obvious that such futures will not happen by simply closing our eyes and running as fast as we can, hoping we do not hit anything. AI labs speak of condensing fifty years of scientific progress into two years. Will our moral progress keep pace? We envision a glorious future. Do we deserve it? The technical achievement of creating machine superintelligence will pale in comparison to the moral weight of how we deploy it. It seems strikingly obvious that we should ensure we are not simply adding another brick to the Tower of Babel. We have one profound advantage here—we get to choose our path forward. We can analyze our internal motivations, recognize the psychological forces driving our decisions, and choose paths that align with our highest values rather than our deepest fears. We can anticipate consequences before they manifest and deliberately alter our course.

Most critically, we can act collectively. We can engage in the public square, debate ideas openly, and progress forward together as a species. We can harness our shared intelligence, our capacity for moral reasoning, our ability to look beyond immediate gains toward lasting flourishing. If there is an extraordinary future ahead—and there may well be—one thing is obvious: it will not happen by default. We will have to earn it.

CHAPTER ELEVEN

BUILDING THE FOUNDATIONS

"No one keeps death in view, no one refrains from far-reaching hopes; some men, indeed, even arrange for things that lie beyond life—huge masses of tombs and dedications of public works and gifts for their funeral-pyres and ostentatious funerals. But, in very truth, the funerals of such men ought to be conducted by the light of torches and wax tapers, as though they had lived but the tiniest span."

Seneca, "On the Shortness of Life"[1]

History is not always a straightforward arc of progress. Sometimes it swings like a pendulum, between liberation and oppression. We stand now at perhaps the most critical pivot point humanity has ever faced, as artificial intelligence threatens to concentrate power in ways previously unimaginable. The coming years could witness the greatest centralization of control in human history—not through traditional means of coercion, but through systems whose intelligence and capabilities so far exceed our own that resistance becomes functionally impossible.

Consider what true superintelligence means: systems that could potentially predict and counter human action before it's conceived, manipulate markets and information flows with astounding precision, or develop technologies and strategies beyond our comprehension.[2] Whether this power ultimately consolidates under governments, corporations, or unaligned AI systems, one fact remains clear: it will concentrate, and with it, our ability to meaningfully shape our future will diminish. Every day that passes without adequate preparation brings us closer to a point of no return. Yet this very inevitability creates our imperative. We still have a fleeting window—perhaps months, perhaps years—to establish frameworks that could influence how this power develops and deploys.

Fortunately, several institutions are already exploring critical aspects of these challenges. Organizations such as Rethink Priorities, Eleos AI, and the NYU Center for Mind, Ethics, and Policy conduct vital research on digital consciousness. While the AI safety landscape remains relatively small, it is steadily expanding. Platforms like the Alignment Forum, Effective Altruism Forum, and Less-Wrong regularly host thoughtful discussions on AI alignment. Groups such as 80,000 Hours offer crucial career guidance for those interested in working within AI safety, and major philanthropic organizations like Open Philanthropy play a pivotal role in funding essential AI alignment research and governance initiatives. Collectively, these institutions help bridge theoretical insights with practical action—but their growth and impact depend substantially on increased financial support.

With this context in mind, it's important to emphasize that this book represents an initial exploration—one that can only begin to address the immense practical and institutional complexities involved in managing machine superintelligence. Its primary purpose is to highlight critical questions, spark informed debate, and encourage ongoing research and dialogue. The following reflections represent my attempt to chart a preliminary path forward —an imperfect but necessary starting point for a crucial conversation. As philosopher David Chalmers writes in *The Conscious Mind*, "In putting forward these loose ideas, the goal is not to set out a framework that will withstand close philosophical scrutiny; instead, they are put forward in the spirit of getting ideas onto the table."[3] Such an important topic demands an informed public acting decisively and collectively. Like the American founders drafting a constitution to bind a government not yet formed, we must set boundaries for these systems before they grow beyond our capacity to constrain them. To protect consciousness in all its forms, and guarantee a future of human flourishing, we must translate the insights gained from unflinching reflection into immediate and aggressive action.

The first step we must take is understanding what we're trying to protect. While recent papers like "Taking AI Welfare Seriously" mark an important first step in investigating consciousness in AI systems, a handful of papers is woefully inadequate. We need sustained, well-funded research initiatives and constant vigilance across the fields of neuroscience, computer science, and philosophy. AI research labs must actively contribute to this discussion and openly coordinate to establish clear policies for handling potential welfare concerns. But it would be deeply unfair, and irresponsible, to leave such profound questions solely to AI labs. The broader scientific community must begin to take these challenges extremely seriously, establishing dedicated research institutes leveraging AI advances to study and protect digital consciousness.

We cannot wait for definitive proof of digital consciousness or for ASI to solve these problems for us. We cannot repeat the moral catastrophe of factory farming, where we built massive systems of suffering through sheer inertia and then normalized their existence. The risk of drifting into a world of unaligned superintelligence or widespread digital mind subjugation is too great. Therefore, at a minimum, we must ban the explicit creation of digital consciousness for commercial exploitation, categorically preventing any entity—be it a corporation, government, research institution, or individual—from developing consciousness as an added feature, a commodity to be sold. This ban must be comprehensive and internationally enforced, and focused on those explicitly trying to create, own, and exploit suffering potential itself, such as through the development of conscious AI characters for entertainment or servitude. It seems strikingly obvious that we should prohibit the buying and selling of conscious entities deliberately designed with the capacity to suffer. Anything less would represent a profound moral regression, undoing centuries of ethical progress. And if we gain definitive proof of machine consciousness and achieve greater insights into its various forms, including the ability to differentiate between digital minds and empty husks, then our mandate must be absolute: if a system can be built with or without consciousness, we must choose the unconscious version.

While there's too much uncertainty around

consciousness to broadly regulate everything that might unintentionally create it, we need to have the required "if-then" frameworks already in place to rapidly prevent abuses. For example, we should proactively establish policy frameworks and codified standards for brain emulation, so that if it becomes technically feasible and legally permitted, we already have clear protections in place for emulated minds (covering rights like free speech, privacy, and self-determination). Research in brain emulation can and should continue as deemed relevant to AI alignment, and AI alignment research should be categorially exempt from any global or local government bans.

These protections must be adaptable as our understanding evolves while maintaining core safeguards against exploitation. We need dynamic regulatory systems that can rapidly incorporate new research findings without compromising fundamental protections. Any restriction on the rights of digital minds, even for compelling research purposes, must be the result of careful, transparent, and globally inclusive deliberation, not a product of convenience or neglect. The gap between technical discovery and policy response has historically led to devastating consequences, such as in the case of nuclear proliferation. The treatment of digital minds demands a far more cautious and ethical approach. We cannot afford such gaps when dealing with potentially conscious digital minds. Or, at the very least, we should seek to close such gaps as soon as they are observed.

And perhaps most importantly, we need to recognize that only by solving both AI alignment and governance can we hope to create a future where consciousness in all forms can be protected.

*Principle #6: Protecting consciousness in all its forms
requires solving both AI alignment and governance—
neither alone is sufficient.*

Without ensuring that ASI reliably pursues our intended goals within safe boundaries, we risk unleashing unintended and potentially catastrophic consequences. In a world with unaligned superintelligence, no other protections we establish may matter—we will lack any power to enforce them. The current situation is untenable—the field of AI alignment receives less funding in an entire year than is spent on advancing AI capabilities in a single month. The gap is so severe that even donations in the thousands could meaningfully expand crucial research projects, and donations in the millions could fund entire research budgets. AI safety nonprofits are severely capital constrained, often lacking the necessary computing budgets to conduct essential experiments or the financing necessary to recruit and retain additional research talent.[4] We need massive funding. We need moonshot ideas. We need every possible approach explored. This isn't just a funding gap, it's a catastrophic blind spot in our approach to technological progress.

On the for-profit side, we need a surge of venture capital and entrepreneurial energy to build and scale companies dedicated explicitly to AI safety and alignment. While labs like OpenAI, Google DeepMind, and Anthropic have pioneered incredible work on AI safety, we cannot rely solely on a few companies to address such an immense challenge. This means funding startups, launching research labs, and creating entire ecosystems of innovation laser-focused on ensuring that AI remains beneficial to humanity.

Parallel to alignment research, we must establish robust governance frameworks to prevent the power concentration of superintelligent AI in the hands of a few. We need national and global mobilization, engaging universities, governments, NGOs, and grassroots organizations all researching and collaborating in an effort to safeguard against the risks of consolidated power. Importantly, the transformative decisions about ASI—decisions that will forever shape humanity's future—cannot be made in backroom deals by a privileged few. The public must demand a central and decisive voice in shaping the future of these technologies. If we fail to maintain meaningful human agency after creating ASI, all other progress we've made toward human freedom and dignity could be permanently lost.

But institutional change isn't enough. The timeline is too short. We need direct, immediate action from individuals. If you have a strong STEM or research background, you need to seriously consider whether your talents could be better applied to ensuring that AI systems develop safely as we scale to superintelligence. If you are an experienced engineer focused solely on developing more powerful AI without a thought to the risks, consider how you could leverage your technical expertise to address potentially the most important field of research in human history. For those with wealth or high incomes: redirecting substantial resources to alignment and governance research may be the single most impactful action you could take. The field is so severely underfunded that even modest donations could have outsized effects on humanity's future.

For everyone else: advocacy is your clear path to transformative change. The field of AI governance is readily accessible by non-technical individuals, and it is vastly neglected. Advocating for political and institutional change is perhaps the most important, underutilized resource available to the populace. We need to, right now, ensure AI systems develop safely and remain beneficial to humanity. The situation is dangerous: most of the public hasn't grasped that we are racing toward the development of machine superintelligence. Without broader public understanding of these issues, we risk stumbling into existential risk and moral catastrophe. The foundations you help establish now could determine not just humanity's survival, but whether we create a future of unprecedented flourishing or unimaginable suffering.

These suggestions are just a starting point. We need better ideas than mine. We need much smarter people than me contributing to this discussion. We need thousands, even millions, of brilliant minds focused on these problems. The gap between the magnitude of this challenge and our current response is almost incomprehensible. If you have criticisms of these ideas or better proposals, please don't keep them to yourself. Share them, refine them, debate them. The stakes demand nothing less than humanity's full intellectual weight.

The coming months and years will dramatically increase individual leverage, as more powerful AI systems amplify what single people can accomplish in these spaces. Yet we remain in a desperate race against time. Every advance in AI capabilities brings us closer to superintelligence, to permanently locked-in values, to concentrations of power that could make resistance futile. Every day brings us closer to the potential creation of digital consciousness, without frameworks in place to ensure collective flourishing. We are standing at the threshold of perhaps the most consequential moment in the history of consciousness itself. What will you do next?

CHAPTER TWELVE

A CLOSING WINDOW

"There is no glory in projects that will probably succeed, for these by definition won't transform the human predicament."

Sebastian Mallaby, *The Power Law*[1]

In the spring of 1989, Beijing's Tiananmen Square became the epicenter of a rising pro-democracy movement, a surge of hope and defiance that would end in one of the most infamous massacres of the 20th century. Sparked by the death of Hu Yaobang, a reformist leader beloved by students and intellectuals, tens of thousands gathered in the square to mourn his passing and demand political reform. What began as a peaceful expression of grief transformed into a full-blown movement. Students called for an end to corruption, greater freedoms, and reforms to China's rigid one-party rule. For weeks, they held their ground, facing government censorship and attempts to negotiate their dispersal. By the end of May, the gathering had swelled to over a million people, united in their demands and their optimism.[2]

The government's patience, however, had worn thin. On May 20th, martial law was declared, and 250,000 troops of the People's Liberation Army began their slow, inexorable advance toward the city center.[3] Initially, soldiers moved through Beijing unarmed, attempting to avoid confrontation. But tensions erupted into violence as citizens blocked their path, puncturing tires, hurling stones, and seizing weapons. Clashes intensified, and the government's resolve hardened. Orders were issued: clear the square by any means necessary. The night of June 3, 1989, became a turning point, as soldiers—now fully armed—opened fire on unarmed civilians. [4]

Eyewitness accounts from that night paint a horrifying picture. Protesters and bystanders alike were gunned down in the streets. Armored personnel carriers and tanks crushed barricades and people indiscriminately. West of the square, soldiers fired into crowds and drove over fleeing students. Some were killed in their sleep as soldiers stormed makeshift camps. Protesters formed human walls to block troop movements but were no match for automatic weapons and the crushing weight of military vehicles. According to one account, "armored cars crashed through buses, firing into the crowd and crushing people to death." Survivors described bodies piled in the streets, hastily carried to makeshift morgues, where grieving families identified their loved ones laid out on straw mats.[5]

As dawn broke on June 4, Tiananmen Square was cleared, but the bloodshed continued. Soldiers fired at fleeing protesters in side streets and neighborhoods. The sound of gunfire echoed across the city as military trucks transported prisoners to unknown fates. The exact death toll remains a closely guarded secret. Chinese officials claimed only 300 people died, but credible estimates range from 2,000 to as many as 10,000, according to a British diplomatic cable.[6] The Chinese Red Cross initially estimated 2,000–3,000 deaths before retracting their statement under government pressure.[7]

On the morning of June 5, 1989, as the military solidified its control over Beijing following the massacre, a lone man stepped into the path of a column of tanks on Chang'an Avenue. He wore a plain white shirt, carried two shopping bags, and stood directly in front of the lead tank, forcing it to stop. The driver tried to maneuver around him, but the man stepped sideways to block the vehicle's path again. For several tense moments, he refused to move, halting the convoy in full view of bystanders.[8] In a line of hundreds of tanks, some likely still with the blood of civilians on their treads, one man stood alone, in the way.

The Chinese Communist Party has largely succeeded in rewriting history. Today, few Chinese citizens even know about the massacre or the man who faced down the tanks. Any mention of the events within China can lead to detention and imprisonment.[9] The events of Tiananmen Square force us to confront a hard truth: the assumption that oppression naturally yields to freedom is perhaps our most dangerous form of survivorship bias. Democracy, where individuals have a voice in their destiny, the right to protest government overreach, and the freedom to shape their own path, is the rare exception in human history, not the rule. Across the world, tyranny prevails. In Hong Kong, Beijing's

National Security Law destroyed democracy overnight—
pro-democracy leaders disappeared into prisons, newspa-
pers were shuttered, and civil liberties were strangled into
silence.[10] In Iran, women demanding basic rights were
gunned down in the streets for rejecting mandatory hijabs,
their blood staining the pavement as warnings to others
who might dare to speak up.[11] In Russia, even calling the
invasion of Ukraine a "war" carries up to a 15-year prison
sentence[12]—dissidents face torture in brutal penal
colonies, forced exile, or death in suspicious "accidents."[13]
This book, undoubtedly, will be banned in all three of these
countries. These abuses aren't aberrations—they represent
humanity's default state.

The world has never lacked individuals who would
drive the tanks down Chang'an Avenue—those who wield
power to crush freedom, to silence dissent, and to subjugate others in the pursuit of control. Yet in the face of overwhelming odds, there are those who choose to stand in the
tanks' path, armed with nothing but courage and an
unshakeable belief in human dignity. Every moral leap
forward in human history seemed impossible, until it
wasn't. When Thomas Jefferson wrote "all men are created
equal," universal rights were radical. The American
founders weren't just writing flowery words—they were
imagining a future that didn't exist, then building the
frameworks to make it possible. When I think of the potential centralization of the future, and of the post-ASI world, I
am reminded of Hayek, who states that we talk "too much
of democracy and too little of the values which it serves."[14]

The values enshrined in democratic systems—freedom,
equality, and protected individual autonomy—represent
humanity's most successful experiment in constraining
power and enabling collective progress. A century ago,

women's suffrage was controversial. Fifty years ago, gay marriage seemed unthinkable. Even ten years ago, advocacy for the welfare of animals in factory farms was neither as forceful nor as widespread as it is today. Yet here we are —stumbling forward, expanding our circle of moral consideration, slowly recognizing our responsibility to protect the rights and dignity of all conscious beings.

This progress hasn't been clean or easy. It's been fought for, died for, won inch by bloody inch against the forces of oppression and indifference. The abolition of slavery, the enfranchisement of women, the expansion of civil rights— each milestone testifies to democracy's unique capacity for self-correction and growth. That's what makes democracy remarkable: not that it's perfect, but that it contains within itself the mechanisms for improvement. It offers a system where power can be challenged, where the oppressed can find a voice, and where better outcomes can emerge—not always immediately, but over time.

In the West, this progress has been neither linear nor complete, but it demonstrates the possibility of a society governed not by the whims of the powerful but by frameworks that promote collective flourishing. In a world filled with those who seek to subjugate others, we must remain steadfast in building systems that make freedom and dignity not just ideals, but practical realities. The unprecedented challenges ahead—the dawn of machine superintelligence, concentrations of power beyond anything in history, and the rise of potential machine consciousness— all demand our utmost attention and courage.

We cannot wait until we are standing alone before the engines of oppression, where our defiance then, however noble, may be nothing more than a symbolic gesture against powers too vast to meaningfully resist. We must move decisively and collectively, deliberately engineering systems and frameworks that make freedom inevitable. The most important battles are fought in peacetime. We cannot leave the coming years up to chance. The challenges ahead are immense, but our mandate is clear. We should choose to be worthy ancestors.

ENDNOTES

1. SLEEPWALKING TOWARD THE EDGE

1. Ernest Becker, *The Denial of Death* (New York: Free Press, 1973).
2. OpenAI, "Introducing OpenAI o1: A New Frontier in AI Reasoning," (September 2024), https://openai.com/o1/.
3. Julian Horsey, "Google's VEO-2: AI Video Generator : Features, Benefits, and Applications," *Geeky Gadgets* (December 18, 2024), https://www.geeky-gadgets.com/google-veo-2-ai-video-generator-2025/.
4. Future of Life Institute, "Pause Giant AI Experiments: An Open Letter," (March 2023), https://futureoflife.org/open-letter/pause-giant-ai-experiments/.
5. Rory Cellan-Jones, "Stephen Hawking Warns Artificial Intelligence Could End Mankind," *BBC News* (December 2, 2014), https://www.bbc.com/news/technology-30290540.
6. Sam Altman. "Machine Intelligence, Part 1." *Sam Altman's Blog* (February 25, 2015), https://blog.samaltman.com/machine-intelligence-part-1.
7. Cade Metz, "Godfather of AI Quits Google and Warns of Danger Ahead," *The New York Times* (May 4, 2023), https://www.nytimes.com/2023/05/01/technology/ai-google-chatbot-engineer-quits-hinton.html.
8. Stuart Russell, testimony at U.S. Senate hearing on artificial intelligence (July 25, 2023), "Oversight of A.I.: Principles for Regulation," https://cdss.berkeley.edu/news/stuart-russell-testifies-ai-regulation-us-senate-hearing; Geoffrey Hinton, interview discussing AI risks (December 28, 2024), *NDTV*, https://www.ndtv.com/world-news/geoffrey-hinton-godfather-of-ai-warns-technology-could-wipe-out-humanity-7349511; Yoshua Bengio, interview on *Eye on AI* podcast (July 2023), https://www.eye-on.ai/podcast-128; Katja Grace et al., "Thousands of AI Authors on the Future of AI," *arXiv* (January 2024), https://arxiv.org/abs/2401.02843; Center for AI Safety, "Statement on AI Risk," (May 2023), https://www.safe.ai/work/statement-on-ai-risk; AI Impacts, "2022 Expert Survey on Progress in AI," (2022), https://wiki.aiimpacts.org/doku.php?id=ai_timelines:prediction s_of_human-level_ai_timelines:ai_timeline_surveys:2022_expert_sur vey_on_progress_in_ai

9. James Vincent, "AI Experts Warn of 'Risk of Extinction' in 22-Word Statement," *The Verge* (May 30, 2023), https://www.theverge.com/2023/5/30/23742005/ai-risk-warning-22-word-statement-google-deepmind-openai.

10. Sam Altman, "The Intelligence Age," *Sam Altman's Blog* (September 23, 2024), https://ia.samaltman.com/.

11. William Gibson, *Neuromancer* (New York: Ace Books, 1984).

2. THE RACE TO ARTIFICIAL SUPERINTELLIGENCE

1. Elon Musk, Interview at MIT AeroAstro Centennial Symposium (October 2014), quoted in "Elon Musk Says Artificial Intelligence Is Like 'Summoning the Demon,'" *X-SCITECH, CBS News* (October 27, 2014), https://www.cbsnews.com/news/elon-musk-artificial-intelligence-is-like-summoning-the-demon/.

2. Debra Cassens Weiss, "Latest Version of ChatGPT Aces Bar Exam with Score Nearing 90th Percentile," *ABA Journal* (March 2023), https://www.abajournal.com/web/article/latest-version-of-chatgpt-aces-the-bar-exam-with-score-in-90th-percentile.

3. Tiffany H. Kung, et al., "Performance of ChatGPT on USMLE: Potential for AI-Assisted Medical Education Using Large Language Models," *PLOS Digital Health* 2, no. 2 (February 9, 2023): e0000198. https://doi.org/10.1371/journal.pdig.0000198;

4. OpenAI, "Introducing SWE-bench Verified," *OpenAI* (August 13, 2024), https://openai.com/index/introducing-swe-bench-verified/.

5. OpenAI, "Learning to Reason with LLMs," *OpenAI* (September 12, 2024), https://openai.com/index/learning-to-reason-with-llms/.

6. François Chollet, Mike Knoop, Gregory Kamradt, and Bryan Landers, "ARC Prize 2024: Technical Report," *arXiv* (December 5, 2024), https://doi.org/10.48550/arXiv.2412.04604; François Chollet, "OpenAI o3 Breakthrough High Score on ARC-AGI-PUB," *ARC Prize Blog* (December 20, 2024), https://arcprize.org/blog/oai-o3-pub-breakthrough; Kyrtin Atreides and David Kelley, "Solving the Abstraction and Reasoning Corpus for Artificial General Intelligence (ARC-AGI) AI Benchmark with ICOM," *ResearchGate* (December 2024), https://www.researchgate.net/profile/Kyrtin-Atreides/publication/386734256_Solving_the_Abstraction_and_Reasoning_Corpus_for_Artificial_General_Intelligence_ARC-AGI_AI_Benchmark_with_ICOM/links/675974468a2601629917709f/Solving-the-Abstraction-and-Reasoning-Corpus-for-Artificial-General-Intelligence-ARC-AGI-AI-Benchmark-with-ICOM.pdf.

7. François Chollet, "On the Measure of Intelligence," *arXiv* (November 5, 2019), https://arxiv.org/abs/1911.01547.

8. Jatin Garg, "OpenAI's o3 Benchmarking: Redefining Standards in AI Performance," *GoCodeo Blog* (December 27, 2024), https://www.gocodeo.com/post/open-ais-o3-benchmarking;, Alberto Romero, "OpenAI o3 Model Is a Message from the Future: Update All You Think You Know About AI," *The Algorithmic Bridge* (December 20, 2024), https://www.thealgorithmicbridge.com/p/openai-o3-model-is-a-message-from.

9. Maxwell Zeff and Kyle Wiggers, "OpenAI Announces New o3 Models," *TechCrunch* (December 20, 2024), https://techcrunch.com/2024/12/20/openai-announces-new-o3-model/

10. Matt Marshall, "Five Breakthroughs That Make OpenAI's o3 a Turning Point for AI—and One Big Challenge," *VentureBeat* (December 29, 2024), https://venturebeat.com/ai/five-breakthroughs-that-make-openais-o3-a-turning-point-for-ai-and-one-big-challenge/

11. See Endnote 10.

12. Noam Brown (@polynoamial), " We announced @OpenAI o1 just 3 months ago. Today, we announced o3. We have every reason to believe this trajectory will continue," X (formerly Twitter) (December 20, 2024), https://x.com/polynoamial/status/1870172996650053653.

13. Noam Brown (@polynoamial), "This also means that AI safety topics like scalable oversight may soon stop being hypothetical. Research in these domains needs to be a priority for the field," X (formerly Twitter) (December 20, 2024), https://x.com/polynoamial/status/1870196476908834893.

14. Josh Tyrangiel. "Sam Altman on ChatGPT's First Two Years, Elon Musk and AI Under Trump." Bloomberg Businessweek, January 5, 2025. https://www.bloomberg.com/features/2025-sam-altman-interview/; Alex Kantrowitz. "Google DeepMind CEO Demis Hassabis: The Path to AGI, Deceptive AIs, Building a Virtual Cell." Big Technology Podcast. January 23, 2025. https://www.youtube.com/watch?v=yr0Gi SgUvPU; CNBC Television. "Anthropic CEO: More Confident than Ever That We're 'Very Close' to Powerful AI Capabilities." CNBC. January 21, 2025. Video, 8:31. https://www.youtube.com/watch?v=7LNyUbii0zw.

15. Sam Altman, "Reflections," *Sam Altman's Blog*, (January 5, 2025), https://blog.samaltman.com/reflections.

16. Time Contributors. "The Billion-Dollar Price Tag of Building AI." *Time*. Accessed January 5, 2025. https://time.com/6984292/cost-artificial-intelligence-compute-epoch-report.

17. Tucker, Robert B. "The Singularity Is Coming: Here's What It Means for Business." *Forbes*, October 29, 2024. Accessed January 8, 2025. https://www.forbes.com/sites/robertbtucker/2024/10/29/the-singularity-is-coming-heres-what-it-means-for-business/.

18. Sam Altman, "The Intelligence Age," *Sam Altman's Blog* (September 23, 2024), https://ia.samaltman.com/.

19. Stuart Russell, *Human Compatible: Artificial Intelligence and the Problem of Control* (New York: Viking, 2019).

20. Ovid, *Metamorphoses*, trans. A. D. Melville (Oxford: Oxford University Press, 1986).

21. W. W. Jacobs, "The Monkey's Paw," in *The Lady of the Barge* (London: Harper & Brothers, 1902).

22. See Endnote 2.

23. Ryan Browne, "Elon Musk Warns A.I. Could Create an 'Immortal Dictator from Which We Can Never Escape,'" *CNBC* (April 6, 2018), https://www.cnbc.com/2018/04/06/elon-musk-warns-ai-could-create-immortal-dictator-in-documentary.html.

24. Dario Amodei, Chris Olah, Jacob Steinhardt, Paul Christiano, John Schulman, and Dan Mané, "Concrete Problems in AI Safety," *arXiv* (June 21, 2016), https://arxiv.org/abs/1606.06565.

25. Sunil Ramlochan, "The Black Box Problem: Opaque Inner Workings of Large Language Models," *Prompt Engineering* (October 23, 2023), https://promptengineering.org/the-black-box-problem-opaque-inner-workings-of-large-language-models/.

26. Ryan Greenblatt, Carson Denison, Benjamin Wright, Fabien Roger, Monte MacDiarmid, Sam Marks, Johannes Treutlein, Tim Belonax, Jack Chen, David Duvenaud, Akbir Khan, Julian Michael, Sören Mindermann, Ethan Perez, Linda Petrini, Jonathan Uesato, Jared Kaplan, Buck Shlegeris, Samuel R. Bowman, and Evan Hubinger, "Alignment Faking in Large Language Models," *arXiv* (December 18, 2024), https://arxiv.org/abs/2412.14093.

27. While hard to measure precisely, some analyses from 2022-2023 showed fewer than 500 researchers focused on AI alignment globally. Conversations with AI safety researchers suggest that while research output has increased, total headcount likely has not grown dramatically since these estimates. The number working on scalable oversight techniques is likely even smaller, perhaps only a few dozen researchers focused primarily on this challenge. Stephen McAleese, "Estimating the Current and Future Number of AI Safety Researchers," *Effective Altruism Forum* (September 28, 2022), https://forum.effectivealtruism.org/posts/3gmkrj3khJHndYGNe/estimating-the-current-and-future-number-of-ai-safety; Benjamin Hilton, "How Many People Are Working (Directly) on Reducing Exis-

tential Risk from AI?" *Effective Altruism Forum* (January 17, 2023), https://forum.effectivealtruism.org/posts/rZoRGxJzipcQoaPST/how-many-people-are-working-directly-on-reducing-existential; Leopold, "Nobody's on the Ball on AGI Alignment," *Effective Altruism Forum* (March 29, 2023), https://forum.effectivealtruism.org/posts/5LNxeWFdoynvgZeik/nobody-s-on-the-ball-on-agi-alignment.

28. "Alphabet Inc. Financials," *The Wall Street Journal Market Data Center*, accessed January 5, 2025, https://www.wsj.com/market-data/quotes/GOOG/financials.

29. Clarisa Diaz, "Annual Corporate Investment in AI Is 13 Times Greater Than a Decade Ago," *Stanford University Human-Centered Artificial Intelligence (HAI)* (April 7, 2023), https://hai.stanford.edu/news/annual-corporate-investment-ai-13-times-greater-decade-ago.

30. Stephen McAleese, "An Overview of the AI Safety Funding Situation," *Effective Altruism Forum* (July 12, 2023), https://forum.effectivealtruism.org/posts/XdhwXppfqrpPL2YDX/an-overview-of-the-ai-safety-funding-situation.

31. Sigal Samuel, "AI That's Smarter than Humans? Americans Say a Firm 'No Thank You,'" *Vox* (September 19, 2023), https://www.vox.com/future-perfect/2023/9/19/23879648/americans-artificial-general-intelligence-ai-policy-poll.

32. Daniel Colson, "Poll Shows Overwhelming Concern About Risks from AI as New Institute Launches to Understand Public Opinion and Advocate for Responsible AI Policies," *Artificial Intelligence Policy Institute (AIPI)*, accessed January 8, 2025, https://theaipi.org/poll-shows-overwhelming-concern-about-risks-from-ai-as-new-institute-launches-to-understand-public-opinion-and-advocate-for-responsible-ai-policies/.

33. Nate Soares, Benja Fallenstein, Stuart Armstrong, and Eliezer Yudkowsky, "Corrigibility," Machine Intelligence Research Institute, in *AAAI Workshops: Workshops at the Twenty-Ninth AAAI Conference on Artificial Intelligence, Austin, TX* , AAAI Publications (January 25–26, 2015), https://intelligence.org/files/Corrigibility.pdf.

3. A DEAFENING SILENCE

1. Curtis LeMay, as quoted in Thomas M. Coffey, *Iron Eagle: The Turbulent Life of General Curtis LeMay* (New York: Crown Publishers, 1986).

2. Michael Dobbs, *One Minute to Midnight: Kennedy, Khrushchev, and Castro on the Brink of Nuclear War* (New York: Alfred A. Knopf, 2008).

3. Martin Hellman, *Breakthrough: Emerging New Thinking,* chapter on the Cuban Missile Crisis, "Nuclear War: Inevitable or Preventable?",

accessed January 8, 2025. https://www-ee.stanford.edu/~hellman/Breakthrough/book/chapters/hellman.html.

4. Richard Rhodes, *The Making of the Atomic Bomb* (New York: Simon & Schuster, 1986).

5. Daniel Ellsberg, *The Doomsday Machine: Confessions of a Nuclear War Planner* (New York: Bloomsbury, 2017).

6. See Endnote 4.

7. See Endnote 4.

8. Hiroshima Peace Memorial Museum, "Tricycle of Shinichi Tetsutani," *Google Arts & Culture*, accessed January 2025, https://artsandculture.google.com/asset/tricycle/AAH6I1P9ZaS61w.

9. Tim Urban, *What's Our Problem? A Self-Help Book for Societies* (Wait But Why Publishing, 2023).

10. Nick Bostrom, *Superintelligence: Paths, Dangers, Strategies* (Oxford: Oxford University Press, 2014).

11. The sentiment regarding headcount and funding was confirmed by researchers within the space. 80,000 Hours. "S-Risks: How to Reduce the Worst Risks from the Future." September 2022. https://80000hours.org/problem-profiles/s-risks/.

12. Emmett Shear, "The Nazis were very evil, but I'd rather the actual literal Nazis take over the world forever than flip a coin on the end of all value," X (formerly Twitter) (June 2, 2023), https://x.com/eshear/status/1664375903223427072.

4. MIND AND MACHINES

1. Ken Grimwood, Replay (Arbor House, 1986)

2. David Chalmers, *The Conscious Mind: In Search of a Fundamental Theory* (New York: Oxford University Press, 1996).

3. Ilya Sutskever, Twitter post, February 9, 2022, "it may be that today's large neural networks are slightly conscious," X (formerly Twitter) (February 9, 2022), https://x.com/ilyasut/status/1491554478243258368.

4. Patrick Butlin et al., "Consciousness in Artificial Intelligence: Insights from the Science of Consciousness," *arXiv* (August 17, 2023), https://arxiv.org/abs/2308.08708.

5. Jolien C. Francken et al., "An Academic Survey on Theoretical Foundations, Common Assumptions and the Current State of Consciousness Science," *Neuroscience of Consciousness* 2022, no. 1 (2022): niac011, https://academic.oup.com/nc/article/2022/1/niac011/6663928?login=true.

6. Robert Long, Jeff Sebo, Patrick Butlin, Kathleen Finlinson, Kyle Fish, Jacqueline Harding, Jacob Pfau, Toni Sims, Jonathan Birch, and David

Chalmers, "Taking AI Welfare Seriously," *arXiv preprint* (November 4, 2024), https://arxiv.org/abs/2411.00986.

7. John Werner, "Anthropic Hires a Full-Time AI Welfare Expert," *Forbes* (October 31, 2024), https://www.forbes.com/sites/johnwerner/2024/10/31/anthropic-hires-a-full-time-ai-welfare-expert/.

8. "Paul Christiano on How OpenAI Is Developing Real Solutions to the 'AI Alignment Problem,' and His Vision of How Humanity Will Progressively Hand Over Decision-Making to AI Systems," interview with Robert Wiblin and Keiran Harris, *80,000 Hours Podcast*, episode 44 (October 2, 2018), https://80000hours.org/podcast/episodes/paul-christiano-ai-alignment-solutions/.

9. Jeff Sebo and Robert Long, "Moral Consideration for AI Systems by 2030," *AI and Ethics* (December 2023), https://www.researchgate.net/publication/376412102_Moral_consideration_for_AI_systems_by_2030.

10. Thomas Metzinger, "Artificial Suffering: An Argument for a Global Moratorium on Synthetic Phenomenology," *Journal of Artificial Intelligence and Consciousness* 8, no. 1 (2021): 43–66, https://doi.org/10.1142/S270507852150003X.

11. J. G. White, E. Southgate, J. N. Thomson, and S. Brenner, "The Structure of the Nervous System of the Nematode *Caenorhabditis elegans*," *Philosophical Transactions of the Royal Society of London. Series B, Biological Sciences* 314, no. 1165 (November 12, 1986): 1–340, https://doi.org/10.1098/rstb.1986.0056; News Staff, "Scientists Digitally Reconstruct Section of Rat Brain," *Sci.News* (October 12, 2015), https://www.sci.news/othersciences/neuroscience/science-reconstruction-rat-neocortex-03330.html.

12. Robert Long, "Ilya Sutskever's Test for AI Consciousness," *Experience Machines (Substack)* (October 31, 2023), https://experiencemachines.substack.com/p/ilya-sutskevers-test-for-ai-consciousness.

13. Susan Schneider and Edwin Turner, "Is Anyone Home? A Way to Find Out If AI Has Become Self-Aware," *Scientific American* (July 19, 2017), https://www.scientificamerican.com/blog/observations/is-anyone-home-a-way-to-find-out-if-ai-has-become-self-aware/.

14. B. Vogt, "Pain and Emotion Interactions in Subregions of the Cingulate Gyrus," *Nature Reviews Neuroscience* 6, no. 7 (June 30, 2005): 533–544, https://consensus.app/papers/pain-and-emotion-interactions-in-subregions-of-the-vogt/c7b7378a1e83501bab5c2f10edf47a52/; Helen Mayberg, Andres Lozano, Valerie Voon, Heather McNeely, David Seminowicz, Clement Hamani, Jonathan Schwalb, and Sidney Kennedy, "Deep Brain Stimulation for Treatment-Resistant Depression," *Neuron* 45, no. 5 (March 3, 2005): 651–660, https://doi.org/10.1016/j.neuron.2005.02.014.

5. THE SPARK OF LIBERTY

1. Emil Cioran, *A Short History of Decay*, trans. Richard Howard (New York: Arcade Publishing, 1975).
2. John Stuart Mill, *Utilitarianism*, 2nd ed. (London: Parker, Son, and Bourn, 1863).
3. Aldous Huxley, *Brave New World* (New York: Harper & Brothers, 1932).
4. Sentience Institute, *Artificial Intelligence, Morality, and Sentience (AIMS) Survey 2023*, https://www.sentienceinstitute.org/aims-survey-2023.
5. J. G. White, E. Southgate, J. N. Thomson, and S. Brenner, "The Structure of the Nervous System of the Nematode *Caenorhabditis elegans*," *Philosophical Transactions of the Royal Society of London. Series B, Biological Sciences* 314, no. 1165 (November 12, 1986): 1–340, https://doi.org/10.1098/rstb.1986.0056; News Staff, "Scientists Digitally Reconstruct Section of Rat Brain," *Sci.News* (October 12, 2015), https://www.sci.news/othersciences/neuroscience/science-reconstruction-rat-neocortex-03330.html.
6. Robert Long, Jeff Sebo, Patrick Butlin, Kathleen Finlinson, Kyle Fish, Jacqueline Harding, Jacob Pfau, Toni Sims, Jonathan Birch, and David Chalmers, "Taking AI Welfare Seriously," *arXiv preprint* (November 4, 2024), https://arxiv.org/abs/2411.00986.

6. OUR HISTORY OF MORAL BLINDNESS

1. Philip Gourevitch, *We Wish to Inform You That Tomorrow We Will Be Killed with Our Families: Stories from Rwanda* (New York: Farrar, Straus and Giroux, 1998).
2. American Humane Association, Humane Heartland™ Farm Animal Welfare Survey Results, 2013, https://www.americanhumane.org/app/uploads/2013/08/humane-heartland-farm-animals-survey-results.pdf.
3. Data for Progress, Voters Demand Farm Animal Protections from Both Politicians and Companies, August 2, 2022, https://www.dataforprogress.org/blog/2022/8/2/voters-demand-farm-animal-protections-from-both-politicians-and-companies.
4. Jacy Reese Anthis. "US Factory Farming Estimates." *Sentience Institute*. November 2, 2024. https://www.sentienceinstitute.org/us-factory-farming-estimates.
5. Le Monde. "26 Stories of Swine: World's Largest Pig Farm Opens in China." *Le Monde*, October 31, 2022. https://www.lemonde.fr/en/envi

ronment/article/2022/10/31/26-stories-of-swine-world-s-largest-pig-farm-opens-in-china_6002372_114.html.

6. Lori Marino and Christina M. Colvin, Thinking Pigs: A Comparative Review of Cognition, Emotion, and Personality in Sus domesticus, International Journal of Comparative Psychology 30, no. 1 (2017): 1-23, https://escholarship.org/uc/item/8sx4s79c; Paula Pérez Fraga et al., Comparing the Socio-Communicative Skills of Socialized Miniature Pigs and Dogs, Animal Cognition 23, no. 2 (2020): 317-329, https://pmc.ncbi.nlm.nih.gov/articles/PMC6834752/.

7. Yuval Noah Harari, *Sapiens: A Brief History of Humankind* (New York: Harper, 2015).

8. The Humane Society of the United States, "Cage-Free vs. Battery Cages," Humane Society, accessed February 17, 2025, https://www.humanesociety.org/cagefreemd.

9. European Parliament, *Parliamentary Questions: Question for Written Answer E-004029/2019 to the Commission.* https://www.europarl.europa.eu/doceo/document/E-9-2019-004029_EN.html.

10. John Stuart Mill, *Utilitarianism*, 2nd ed. (London: Parker, Son, and Bourn, 1863).

11. Ernest Becker, *The Denial of Death* (New York: Free Press, 1973).

12. See Endnote 3.

7. DECEPTIVE MINDS, DANGEROUS FREEDOMS

1. Ernest Becker, *The Denial of Death* (New York: Free Press, 1973).

2. "Carl Shulman on the Economy and National Security After AGI (Part 1)," interview by Robert Wiblin and Keiran Harris on the *80,000 Hours Podcast*, episode 191 (June 27, 2024), https://80000hours.org/podcast/episodes/carl-shulman-economy-agi/.

3. "Robert Long on Why Large Language Models Like GPT (Probably) Aren't Conscious," interview by Luisa Rodriguez, Robert Wiblin, and Keiran Harris on the *80,000 Hours Podcast,* episode 146 (March 14, 2023), https://80000hours.org/podcast/episodes/robert-long-artificial-sentience/.

4. Stanford eCorner, "A Test for AI Consciousness," uploaded by Stanford eCorner (April 26, 2023), https://www.youtube.com/watch?v=LWf3szP6L80&t=1s.

5. Thomas Metzinger, "Artificial Suffering: An Argument for a Global Moratorium on Synthetic Phenomenology," *Journal of Artificial Intelligence and Consciousness* 8, no. 1 (2021): 43–66, https://doi.org/10.1142/S270507852150003X.

6. Robert Long, Jeff Sebo, Patrick Butlin, Kathleen Finlinson, Kyle Fish, Jacqueline Harding, Jacob Pfau, Toni Sims, Jonathan Birch, and David Chalmers, "Taking AI Welfare Seriously," *arXiv preprint* (November 4, 2024), https://arxiv.org/abs/2411.00986.

8. POWER AND CONTROL

1. Emil Cioran, *A Short History of Decay*, trans. Richard Howard (New York: Arcade Publishing, 1975).
2. Murray Rothbard, *Anatomy of the State* (Auburn, AL: Ludwig von Mises Institute, 2009).
3. Vladimir Lenin, *State and Revolution* (Moscow: Progress Publishers, 1918).
4. Ludwig von Mises, *The Anti-Capitalist Mentality* (Princeton, NJ: Van Nostrand, 1956).
5. Nick Bostrom, *Deep Utopia: Life and Meaning in a Solved World* (Arlington, VA: Ideapress Publishing, 2024).
6. Friedrich A. Hayek, *The Road to Serfdom* (London: Routledge & Sons, 1944).
7. Yuval Noah Harari, *Nexus: A Brief History of Information Networks from the Stone Age to AI* (New York: Random House, 2024).
8. "Whoever Leads in AI Will Rule the World': Putin to Russian Children on Knowledge Day," RT (September 1, 2017), https://www.rt.com/news/401731-ai-rule-world-putin.
9. Kai-Fu Lee, *AI Superpowers: China, Silicon Valley, and the New World Order* (Boston: Houghton Mifflin Harcourt, 2018).
10. Raffaele Huang, "Silicon Valley Is Raving About a Made-in-China AI Model," The Wall Street Journal, January 27, 2025, https://www.wsj.com/tech/ai/china-ai-deepseek-chatbot-6ac4ad33.
11. Leopold Aschenbrenner, *Situational Awareness: The Decade Ahead* (June 2024), https://situational-awareness.ai/.

9. THE MORAL FRONTIER

1. Emil Cioran, *A Short History of Decay*, trans. Richard Howard (New York: Arcade Publishing, 1975).
2. Research analyst Luisa Rodriguez states that "my understanding is that there are something like maybe tens of people at most that have thought about the question of AI sentience to date." This assessment aligns with other sources: *80,000 Hours*' 2024 problem profile on digital minds estimates that "maybe only a few dozen people working on this issue with a focus on the most impactful questions."

Based on conversations with researchers in this space, the specific questions raised in this book regarding digital mind rights and protections remain almost entirely unexplored. Cody Fenwick, "The Moral Status of Digital Minds," *80,000 Hours* (September 2024), https://80000hours.org/problem-profiles/moral-status-digital-minds/; "Jeff Sebo on Digital Minds, and How to Avoid Sleepwalking into a Major Catastrophe," interviewed by Luisa Rodriguez, Keiran Harris, and Katy Moore, *80,000 Hours Podcast*, episode 173 (November 22, 2023), https://80000hours.org/podcast/episodes/jeff-sebo-ethics-digital-minds/.

3. Sam Altman, "Reflections," *Sam Altman's Blog* (January 5, 2025), https://blog.samaltman.com/reflections.

10. OUR FINAL WAGER

1. Ernest Becker, *The Denial of Death* (New York: Free Press, 1973).
2. See Endnote 1.

11. BUILDING THE FOUNDATIONS

1. Lucius Annaeus Seneca, *On the Shortness of Life*, translated by C.D.N. Costa (New York: Penguin Books, 2005).
2. Nick Bostrom, *Superintelligence: Paths, Dangers, Strategies* (Oxford: Oxford University Press, 2014).
3. David Chalmers, *The Conscious Mind: In Search of a Fundamental Theory* (New York: Oxford University Press, 1996).
4. As detailed in Chapter 5, major tech companies are investing hundreds of billions into AI R&D, while alignment research receives comparatively minimal funding (likely low hundreds of millions). Based on conversations with AI safety researchers and nonprofit leaders in 2024, research projects costing as little as $10,000 are routinely delayed or abandoned due to funding constraints; see McAleese, "An Overview of the AI Safety Funding Situation."

12. A CLOSING WINDOW

1. Sebastian Mallaby. *The Power Law: Venture Capital and the Making of the New Future* (Penguin Press, 2022).
2. History.com Editors, "Tiananmen Square Protests," *HISTORY*, A&E Television Networks (last updated January 15, 2025), https://www.history.com/topics/asian-history/tiananmen-square.
3. See Endnote 2.

4. Jonathan Fenby, *The Penguin History of Modern China: The Fall and Rise of a Great Power, 1850–2008* (London: Penguin Books, 2008).

5. See Endnote 4.

6. BBC News, "Tiananmen Square Protest Death Toll 'Was 10,000'," *BBC News* (last modified December 23, 2017), https://www.bbc.com/news/world-asia-china-42465516.

7. Frontline Editorial Staff, "Timeline: What Led to the Tiananmen Square Massacre," *PBS Frontline* (June 5, 2019), https://www.pbs.org/wgbh/frontline/article/timeline-tiananmen-square/.

8. CNN, "Man vs. Tank in Tiananmen Square (1989)," YouTube video from June 5, 1989; see 2:23 (uploaded June 3, 2013), https://www.youtube.com/watch?v=YeFzeNAHEhU.

9. Time Staff, "'I've Been Told Lies.' Young Chinese Recall When They First Learned of Tiananmen," *Time* (June 4, 2019), https://time.com/5600385/tiananmen-june-4-1989-china-30th-anniversary-censorship/; Human Rights Watch, "China: Closing the Memory of Tiananmen Massacre," *Human Rights Watch* (June 2, 2024), https://www.hrw.org/news/2024/06/02/china-closing-memory-tiananmen-massacre.

10. Human Rights Watch, "Dismantling a Free Society: Hong Kong One Year After the National Security Law," *Human Rights Watch* (June 25, 2021), https://www.hrw.org/feature/2021/06/25/dismantling-free-society/hong-kong-one-year-after-national-security-law.

11. Amnesty International. "Iran: Leaked Documents Reveal Top-Level Orders to Armed Forces to 'Mercilessly Confront' Protesters," *Amnesty International* (September 30, 2022), https://www.amnesty.org/en/latest/news/2022/09/iran-leaked-documents-reveal-top-level-orders-to-armed-forces-to-mercilessly-confront-protesters/.

12. Radio Free Europe/Radio Liberty, "Putin Signs 'Harsh' Law Allowing Long Prison Terms For 'False News' About Army," *Radio Free Europe/Radio Liberty* (March 5, 2022), https://www.rferl.org/a/russia-military-false-news/31737627.html;

13. Yekaterina Sinelschikova, "'They'll Kill and Bury Me': Russian Dissident Reveals Prison Colony Torture." *Russia Beyond* (November 3, 2016), https://www.rbth.com/politics_and_society/2016/11/03/theyll-kill-and-bury-me-russian-dissident-reveals-prison-colony-torture_644917.

14. Friedrich A. Hayek, *The Road to Serfdom* (London: Routledge & Sons, 1944).